Ayurvedic Cooking

Made Easy

Ayurvedic Cooking
Made Easy

100+ Recipes for a Healthy You

Everyday meals to soothe, refresh, and energize your mind and body

Ayurvedic approach

Kumuda Reddy, M.D.
Janardhan Reddy, M.D.
Bonita Pedersen

Samhita Productions
P.O. Box 2164
Kensington, Maryland 20891-2164
Web site: www.allhealthyfamily.com
1 866 ReddyMD
(1 866 733-3963) or
301 770-0610

To Maharishi Mahesh Yogi, Founder of the Transcendental Meditation and TM-Sidhi programs and Maharishi Vedic Medicine.

Acknowledgments

We would like to thank Vaidyas Suhas and Manisha Kshirsagar, Dr. Robert Keith Wallace and Samantha Wallace, and Dr. Edwards Smith for their support and advice. We would also like to thank Laura Wysong for editing, Trix Rosen for the cover photograph, and John Steventon of Ka Concepts for the cover design. We would also like to thank Sarah J. Gallogly and Martin Rowe of Lantern Books for their continuing advice and support.

Contents

INTRODUCTION

Dear Reader,

Welcome to the Vedic way of cooking and eating! This approach to diet comes from Maharishi Vedic MedicineSM, the most complete system of natural holistic health care. I think you will be delightfully surprised to learn that, in this system, food needs to be delicious and satisfying in order to create good health. The recipes included here are very tasty as well as good for you.

Food holds a special place of importance in Maharishi Vedic Medicine. It is considered to be the intelligence of nature in material form. When we eat good food, it enlivens our body's inner intelligence, and this is one of the most powerful things we can do to prevent and treat disease.

As a doctor trained in Maharishi Vedic Medicine, I know that everyone has different needs. Some people need a diet that balances Vata, while others need a diet that balances Pitta or Kapha. (To learn more about Vata, Pitta and Kapha, see the following section.)

The recipes in Section Two are designed to balance Vata in particular. Use these recipes when you show signs of a Vata imbalance (such as anxiety, restlessness, fatigue, dry skin, irregular digestion, constipation, and light, interrupted sleep) or when your doctor has recommended a Vata-pacifying diet. They can also be used by everyone during Vata season, which is the coldest and driest time of the year, generally November through February.

Vata recipes are soothing and calming for your mind and body. They emphasize the sweet, sour and salty tastes, and foods that are heavy, unctuous (oily) and warm in quality.

The recipes in Section Three are designed to balance Pitta in particular. Use these recipes when you show signs of a Pitta imbalance (such as irritability, anger, frustration, excess body heat, acid stomach, skin rashes, and a tendency to be too demanding or critical) or when your doctor has recommended a Pitta-pacifying diet. They can also be used by everyone during Pitta season, which is the hottest time of the year, generally July through October.

Pitta recipes are cooling and refreshing for your mind and body. They emphasize the sweet, bitter and astringent tastes, and foods that are heavy, unctuous (oily) and cool in quality.

The recipes in Section Four are designed to balance Kapha in particular. Use these recipes when you show signs of a Kapha imbalance (such as congestion, overweight, slow digestion, excess sleeping, lethargy, depression, and very oily hair or skin) or when your doctor has recommended a Kapha-pacifying diet. They can also be used by everyone during Kapha season, which is the cold damp time of the year, generally March through June.

Kapha recipes are stimulating and invigorating for your mind and body. They emphasize the pungent, bitter and astringent tastes, and foods that are light, hot and dry in quality.

One of the main tenets of Vedic cooking is that all six tastes—sweet, sour, salty, pungent, bitter and astringent—should be included in every main meal. You will find all six tastes represented in these recipes, in a proportion that is balancing for each dosha.

All the recipes are lacto-vegetarian, which is the healthiest diet for humans to eat according to the Vedic tradition. In addition, favor warm, freshly cooked food rather than cold, raw food because cooked food is easier for the body to digest. Avoid leftovers, fast foods, packaged foods with additives and preservatives, and genetically engineered foods.

Organically grown, freshly prepared food is the best because it contains the fullest value of nature's intelligence. This is what our bodies need to thrive.

Many of you will say that you don't have time to cook like this. But remember the old saying, "Where there's a will, there's a way." You can make a delicious, one-pot meal in a crockpot and pack it in a thermos to take to school or work. Supplement it with fruit and bread, and you will have a tasty, satisfying meal. It may take a little planning, but you'll find that it's well worth it. You'll notice how much better you feel, how much clearer and more energetic, when you eat the Vedic way.

My purpose in bringing out these recipes is to make it easy for you to try this system. Have fun with it! After all, the goal of eating is to create more bliss in the mind and body. You will know you are on the right track when you feel more and more blissful.

The Vedic texts tell us that food is Brahman, the totality. May you enjoy wholeness in life and the benefits of a healthy diet for your entire life.

With warm wishes,
Dr. Kumuda Reddy

What Are Vata, Pitta and Kapha?

Vata, Pitta and Kapha are the three organizing principles of nature, or doshas. They govern the flow of the body's inner intelligence and are responsible for maintaining a healthy balance in the body. The story of the three doshas is part of a much bigger story about the origins of the material universe.

According to the Vedic tradition of knowledge, the basis of creation is an unmanifest field of pure consciousness, or pure intelligence. In modern physics, this is known as the unified field, the source of all the forces and particles in nature. In both Vedic science and modern science, this fundamental field of nature is described as self-referral—in other words, it refers to itself alone in the process of creation. In both traditions, creation occurs spontaneously, according to the very nature of pure consciousness, the unified field.

In the process of unity becoming diversity, Vata, Pitta and Kapha are among the first manifestations. The only levels of life more elemental than the three doshas are *ahamkara* or ego, *buddhi* or intellect, *manas* or mind. Eventually, matter manifests in the form of the five *mahabhutas* —space, air, fire, water and earth.

The five mahabhutas combine into the three physical principles known as the doshas, which are the governing principles of the body. Vata comes from the combination of space and air. It is "airy" by nature. Pitta comes from fire and water and is "fiery" by nature. Kapha comes from the combination of water and earth and is "earthy" by nature.

Governing the Flow of the Body's Inner Intelligence

Vata, Pitta and Kapha are responsible for all the different functions of our minds as well as our bodies.

Vata is the leader of the doshas. It is the only moving principle, so wherever there is any kind of movement in the mind or body, Vata is at work. It governs breathing, blood circulation, elimination, sensory perception, neuromuscular activity, and the quick movement of our thoughts and feelings.

Pitta manages digestion, metabolism and all processes of transformation in the mind and body. It keeps bodily heat in balance and regulates hunger and thirst. It controls how we metabolize our sensory perceptions and how we discriminate between right and wrong. Pitta, when in balance, keeps us happy and contented.

Kapha is responsible for structure and fluid balance. It controls bodily growth and the formation of tissues. It gives solidity and strength to the body and keeps our lungs and joints well lubricated. Kapha also supports feelings of loyalty, affection, forgiveness and courage.

Everyone has all three doshas, always working together. Ideally, they work in perfect harmony and balance, but often our habits of eating and living result in the development of certain imbalances. If these imbalances are not corrected, they will manifest as symptoms of discomfort and disease.

How to Correct Imbalances

The recipes in this book will help correct imbalances. They are not a substitute for proper medical care. For medical recommendations, you must see a physician who is trained in Maharishi Vedic Medicine.

A physician trained in this approach will recommend many different ways to create balance. In addition to diet, there are therapies using the mind, body, behavior and environment. All of these therapies help enliven the body's inner intelligence.

The most profound way to create balance is through the Transcendental Meditation® (TM®) technique because this technique gives the direct experience of pure consciousness, the most basic level of life. Practicing the TM technique is like "watering the root" of the tree of life — all aspects are nourished simultaneously.

Over 600 scientific research studies conducted at more than 200 universities and research institutions in 30 countries around the world have documented the beneficial effects of the TM technique. For more information on how to learn this technique or how to find a doctor trained in Maharishi Vedic Medicine, see page 116.

According to the Vedic tradition, we are truly cosmic. The same laws of nature that structure and maintain the entire universe structure and maintain our own physiology. This truth has been verified by modern science and is described beautifully by Professor Tony Nader, M.D., Ph.D., in his book *Human Physiology: Expression of Veda and the Vedic Literature* (Maharishi Vedic University Press, 1994).

Maharishi Vedic Medicine helps each of us realize our cosmic status: Aham Brahmasmi — "I am totality." Creating balance in the three doshas through proper diet is a powerful way to enliven this totality of Natural Law in our daily lives.

More about Vata

The following list summarizes some of the characteristics of Vata, both in balance and out of balance, and some of the common causes of imbalance.

Vata in balance:
vibrant, lively
flexible, creative, resilient
clear and alert mind
imaginative, sensitive
regular digestion
normal elimination
comfortable monthly cycle
sound sleep
physical stamina is constant

Vata out of balance:
restless, unsettled
anxious, worried
light, interrupted sleep
easily fatigued
underweight
irregular digestion, cramping, gas
constipation
menstrual problems or lower back pain
intolerance of cold weather
dry or rough skin

What causes an imbalance in Vata:
irregular routine
staying up late at night
excessive mental work
traveling, moving
accident, injury, surgery
emotional trauma, grief
improper diet
cold, dry weather

Food Guidelines for Balancing Vata

Favor	Reduce
sweet, sour, salty tastes	pungent, bitter, astringent tastes
warm, heavy, unctuous (oily) qualities	light, cold, dry qualities
all dairy products	
all sweeteners	
ghee and all kinds of oil	
rice, wheat	barley, buckwheat, corn, millet, rye, oats
sweet, sour, heavy fruits such as: avocados, bananas, berries, cherries, dates, grapes, mangoes, melons, oranges, peaches, plums, pineapples, etc.	light, dry fruits such as: apples, cranberries, dried fruits, berries, pears, pomegranates, etc.
almost all vegetables, well cooked with a little oil and Vata-balancing spices (favor asparagus, beets, carrots, cucumbers, green beans, sweet potatoes)	raw vegetables, cabbage, sprouts
all nuts and seeds	all meat, especially red meat
mung dal, red lentils, tofu	all beans, except those listed

More about Pitta

The following list summarizes some of the characteristics of Pitta, both in balance and out of balance, and some of the common causes of imbalance.

Pitta in balance:
energetic, efficient, enterprising
enjoys meeting challenges
articulate and precise in speech
sharp intellect
warm, loving, contented
hearty appetite and good digestion
normal heat and thirst mechanisms
lustrous complexion

Pitta out of balance:
acne, rashes, skin sensitivities
prematurely gray or thinning hair
irritable, angry, impatient
demanding, critical, perfectionist
tends to be workaholic
heartburn, acid stomach
sensitive eyes, visual problems
excessive body heat
finds hot weather unbearable

What causes an imbalance in Pitta:
hot weather or over-exposure to the sun
skipping meals, especially lunch
time pressure, stressful deadlines
too many activities or overwork
alcohol, smoking, food toxins
toxic entertainment
improper diet

Food Guidelines for Balancing Pitta

Here are a few general guidelines to keep in mind when balancing Pitta.

Favor	Reduce
sweet, bitter, astringent tastes	salty, sour, pungent tastes
unctuous (oily) and moderately heavy qualities	light, hot, dry qualities
milk, butter, sweet *lassi* (yogurt drink)	cheese, cultured milk products (except for yogurt in *lassi*)
all sweeteners, except those listed	honey, molasses
ghee, coconut, olive and sunflower oils	almond, corn and sesame oils
white rice, wheat, barley, oats	corn, millet, brown rice, rye
sweet, ripe fruits such as: apples, avocados, cherries, coconut, grapes, mangoes, melons, pears, pomegranates, sweet plums, sweet pineapples, dates, figs, etc.	sour or unripe fruits such as: bananas, berries, cranberries, grapefruits, olives, papayas, peaches, persimmons, sour pineapple, etc.
asparagus, broccoli, pumpkin, Brussels sprouts, cabbage, cauliflower, celery, cucumbers, green beans, leafy greens, potato, sweet potato, zucchini	beets, carrots, hot peppers, garlic, onions, radishes, tomatoes, eggplant
coconut, pumpkin seeds, sunflower seeds	all nuts and seeds, except those listed
garbanzo beans, mung dal, soybeans, and tofu	all beans, except those listed
	all meat, fish, and egg yolks

More about Kapha

The following list summarizes some of the characteristics of Kapha, both in and out of balance, and some of the common causes of imbalance.

Kapha in balance:
practical, down-to-earth
solid, powerful build
physically strong, with vitality and stamina
natural resistance to disease
healthy joints
good memory
tranquil, settled mind
affectionate, kind, forgiving
full of dignity and courage

Kapha out of balance:
respiratory problems such as asthma
excess mucus, sinus congestion, allergies
oily hair and skin
slow digestion, weight gain
excessive sleep
poor sense of taste or smell
loose, stiff or painful joints
complacent, dull, lethargic, depressed
overly possessive, unable to accept change
intolerant of the cold and damp

What causes an imbalance in Kapha:
overeating
eating too many sweet, heavy or oily foods
build-up of toxins in the body
oversleeping
insufficient exercise
not enough variety or activity in life
cold, wet weather

Food Guidelines for Balancing Kapha

Here are a few general guidelines to keep in mind when balancing Kapha.

Favor	Reduce
pungent, bitter, astringent tastes	sweet, sour, salty tastes
light, dry, warm qualities	heavy, unctuous (oily) cold qualities
low-fat milk or diluted whole milk, always boiled before drinking	all dairy products except milk
honey	all sweetners except honey
small amounts of ghee, almond corn or sunflower oils	all oils except those listed
barley, corn, millet, buckwheat, rye	large quantities of wheat, rice or oats
light, dry fruits such as: apricots, cranberries, dried pomegranates, persimmons, etc.	heavy, juicy, sweet or sour fruits such as: apples, bananas, coconuts, dates, figs, etc.
all vegetables, except those listed favor asparagus, eggplant green leafy vegetables, radishes	sweet or juicy vegetables cucumbers, sweet potatoes summer squash, tomatoes
pumpkin seed, sunflower seeds	all nuts and seeds, except those listed
all beans, except tofu	tofu
	all meat and fish

Special Ingredients

Some of the ingredients used in Ayurvedic cooking may not be available at your local grocery store. Find an Indian, Asian, gourmet or health food store that offers the following special items.

Spices:

Asafoetida (also called hing): a dried, powdered resin with a strong taste and smell resembling garlic. It is often combined with rice or wheat flour to soften its flavor, and gum arabic to prevent lumping. Different brands vary in strength, so use sparingly until you are familiar with each brand. Asafoetida can be used as a substitute for onion and garlic.

Cardamom: clusters of small black seeds encased in a green or white pod. The pods can be used whole or the seeds removed and coarsely crushed or powdered. Frequently used in sweets.

Coriander: round, ridged seeds that can be used whole, crushed, or powdered. Coriander is one of the few spices that is good for balancing Pitta because of its sweet, cooling qualities.

Cumin: a brown seed similar in shape and size to caraway, but different in flavor. Can be used whole, crushed or ground into a powder. Used often in Vedic cooking, it is good for balancing all three doshas.

Fennel: the feathery fronds, stalks, bulb and seeds of this vegetable are all used in Vedic cooking and taste a little like licorice. Fennel is primarily sweet in flavor. It is good for balancing both Vata and Pitta.

Fenugreek: a legume, but so flavorful that it is used as a spice, either whole or ground. Primarily bitter and hot in taste, it is helpful for balancing Kapha.

Fresh ginger root: gently warming, good for digestion

and healthful in many ways, fresh ginger figures prominently in Vedic cooking. Seek out organic ginger root for its more delicate flavor.

Black mustard seeds: sautéed whole in ghee, black mustard seeds provide a pungent, sharp flavor to many dishes. They are different from the more common yellow mustard seeds, which are rarely used in Vedic cooking.

Poppy seeds: tiny seeds that are good for balancing both Vata and Pitta. They come in different colors, depending on the color of the poppy flower. In India, poppy seeds are white. In the West, poppy seeds are generally blue-gray or reddish-brown.

Saffron threads: hand-picked stigmas from the saffron crocus flower. Saffron has a sweet flavor and fragrance and is good for balancing all three doshas. Saffron is often soaked in hot water for five or ten minutes to bring out its full value.

Black salt: a mined salt that contains trace minerals and iron, with a distinct taste almost like sulfur. Excellent for digestion.

Rock salt: also contains many minerals that ordinary table salt does not. It comes from dry underground sea beds.

Turmeric: a bright yellow powder that is astringent and bitter in taste. Used frequently in Vedic cooking because it balances all three doshas when used in moderation. Also used as a blood purifier and a tonic for the skin. Be careful when handling turmeric because it stains.

Fresh Herbs:

Cilantro (also called fresh coriander): flavorful green leaves that are often used as a garnish in Vedic cooking. They are bitter, astringent and slightly pungent in taste. They are excellent for balancing Pitta.

Curry leaves: similar in shape to bay leaves but different in flavor. Like bay leaves, they are added whole to various dishes, but not eaten. They can be used fresh, dried or ground into a powder.

Mint leaves: fresh and cooling, mint leaves are perfect for pacifying Pitta. Try them in a variety of dishes—vegetables, grains, salads, chutneys, desserts and freshly made yogurt drinks.

Beans/Peas/Lentils (also called *Dal*):

Aduki beans: reddish-brown beans native to Japan and China. Mild in flavor, they help balance both Pitta and Kapha. Aduki beans can be used in place of mung beans in almost any recipe, but they must be soaked overnight first. They also take longer to cook.

Chana dal: a relative of chickpeas, chana dal is one of the most popular and nutritious beans used in Vedic cooking.

Brown lentils: the most common type of lentil, used in cuisines around the world.

Masoor dal or red lentils: tiny orange lentils that turn golden when cooked. Good for balancing Vata and Kapha.

Whole green mung beans (also called green gram): dark green beans that are extremely nourishing and good for balancing all three doshas.

Split hulled mung beans: small and golden yellow, these are whole green mung beans that have been skinned and split. They are considered the best beans for everyone to eat on a daily basis, and are especially good for young children, the elderly, invalids, and those recuperating from an operation or illness. Split hulled mung beans cook quickly, are easy to digest, and have a light flavor that can be enhanced in multiple ways.

Urad dal (also called black gram): another easy-to-cook, easy-to-digest bean that is used frequently in Vedic cooking. It's a close relative of mung beans, black in color, and very rich in protein. Used whole and unhulled as well as split and skinned, it is good for balancing Vata and Kapha.

Grains:

Barley: one of the best grains for balancing Kapha. Look for organic, whole-grain hulled barley (rather than pearled barley) for the best flavor and nutrition. Makes a low-gluten flour that is often mixed with other flours to make flatbread. Basmati rice: long, slender, whole grains of rice with superb flavor and fragrance. Look for basmati that has been aged at least a year; this will have the best flavor. White basmati is considered the best grain for almost everyone to eat. Brown basmati is also good, but white is easier to digest. Millet: another grain that is very balancing for Kapha. Quinoa: a tiny, power-packed grain that has more protein than any other grain. (Surprisingly, it is pronounced "keen-wa.")

Wheat berries: these whole wheat grains are fresher and contain more nutrients than either processed wheat or wheat flours. Wheat berries need to be cooked longer than most other grains.

Flours:

Chapati flour: a low-gluten, soft-textured wheat flour made from whole wheat kernels and milled to a very fine texture. Ideal for making flatbread doughs.

Chickpea flour (also called *besan*): made from roasted chana dal and used in a variety of ways, including savory snacks and sweet desserts.

Rice flour: often mixed with other flours to make flatbreads or pancakes. For the kind of white rice flour used in these recipes, look in Indian grocery stores (rather than Chinese grocery stores, which carry a different kind of rice flour).

Urad dal flour: made from urad dal beans, this flour is particularly light and delicate in flavor. Often used in making dosas and other flatbreads.

Other Special Ingredients:

Dried unsweetened shredded coconut: one of the best ingredients for balancing Pitta because it is sweet and cooling. Avoid processed coconut that has been sweetened and treated with chemicals to stay soft.

Raw (uncooked) honey: wonderful for balancing Kapha because it is both heating and astringent. Look for honey that is clearly labeled "raw" or "uncooked" because most honey has been processed using heat and this makes it toxic and indigestible. For the same reason, never use honey for baking, and add honey to tea and desserts only when they have cooled enough to eat or drink.

Rose water: made from rose petals and water in a distillation process, with no alcohol added. Very balancing for Pitta because of its cooling properties. Usually added at the end of cooking to desserts, or to flavor sweet beverages.

Sesame seeds: ideal for balancing Vata, because they are sweet, heating, and unctuous (oily). Use white hulled sesame seeds or brown unhulled sesame seeds, according to your preference, but dry-roast them first to bring out their full flavor and value. Roasted sesame seeds are often ground into a powder and mixed with salt to sprinkle on dishes at the table.

Maharishi Ayur-Veda™ Products:

The following products are available from Maharishi Ayurveda Products International, Inc., 1068 Elkton Drive, Colorado Springs, Colorado 80907. Phone: 800-255-8332. Fax: 719-260-7400. E-mail: info@mapi.com. Web site: www.mapi.com.

Spice Mixtures:

Vata Churna™: contains cumin, ginger, fenugreek, turmeric, turbinado sugar, salt and asafoetida in a rice flour base.

Pitta Churna™: contains coriander, fennel, cumin,

turbinado sugar, cardamom, ginger, turmeric, cinnamon and salt.

Kapha Churna™: contains ginger, pepper, coriander, turbinado sugar, turmeric, salt and cinnamon.

Condiments:

Apple Chutney: contains apples, sugar, tamarind paste, salt, lemon juice, ginger, hing, cumin seeds, mustard seeds, cinnamon, cloves and black pepper.

Mango Chutney: contains mangoes, dates, organic evaporated cane juice, salt, lemon, water, ginger, cumin, brown mustard seeds, cloves and cardamom.

Peach Chutney: contains peaches, organic evaporated cane juice, water, raisins, lemon juice, fresh ginger, salt, coriander, cinnamon and cardamom.

Ghee: a healthy gourmet cooking oil that is made from sweet butter.

Flavored Ghees:
Ghee with the addition of natural flavorings.
Ghee with Cinnamon
Ghee with Garlic
Ghee with Garlic and Rosemary
Ghee with Garlic, Fennel and Basil
Ghee with Lemon, Dill and Thyme

Ginger Preserve: a sweet, spicy preserve that stimulates digestion. Contains certified organic evaporated cane juice, ginger, water, lemon purée, modified food starch, lemon peel granules and salt.

Rose Petal Conserve: a sweet, cooling confection. Contains evaporated organic cane juice, rose petals, pectin and citric acid. Especially balancing for Pitta.

Cashew Delight™: a nourishing nut butter treat. Contains cashews roasted in sunflower oil, unrefined dried sugar cane juice, raisins, ghee, whole milk powder, cardamom, asparagus root, winter cherry and lemon oil.

Beverages:

Vata® Tea: contains licorice, ginger, cardamom and cinnamon.

Pitta® Tea: contains cardamom, licorice, ginger, cinnamon and organic dried rose petals.

Kapha® Tea: contains ginger, cloves, pepper, cardamom, turmeric and saffron.

Raja's Cup™: a coffee substitute containing four herbs-clearing nut, kasmard, licorice and winter cherry.

Almond Energy Drink: contains raw sugar, almonds, poppy seeds, winter cherry, herpestis monnieria, cardamom and essence of caldera.

Tips for Beginners

For those unfamiliar with Ayurvedic cooking, a few comments may be helpful. The biggest challenge for most beginners is learning how to handle various Ayurvedic spices. Most recipes call for sautéing spices in hot ghee or oil, which brings out the full flavor and nutritional value of the spices. However, use caution when frying. Whole seeds may spatter, and powdered spices burn easily. Have everything you need close at hand, and be alert to lower the heat or remove the pan from the stove if necessary.

Here are some general guidelines. Mustard seeds and fenugreek seeds need more heat, so sauté them first. Wait until the mustard seeds start to pop, then add other seeds and fresh ginger, which don't require as much heat. Add powdered spices last, because they require only a few seconds to bring out their full flavor. When a recipe calls for sautéed coconut, add the coconut last and stir it continuously, because it burns quickly.

Salt is generally added at the end of cooking so that it won't interfere with the cooking process. If salt is added earlier, its sharp, penetrating quality changes the properties of the different foods and in some cases adds to the cooking time.

Sometimes a recipe calls for dry-roasting a particular spice. The way to do this is by preheating a heavy-bottomed pan on top of the stove; then add the spice. Stir or shake the spice around, and continue roasting over heat until the full fragrance of the spice is released, usually about 30 to 60 seconds. Then add the spice to your dish.

Nuts, grains and seeds can be dry-roasted too. This makes them lighter and easier to digest. You can dry-roast small quantities on top of the stove, stirring continuously to prevent burning, or spread larger quantities on a baking sheet in the oven (preheated to 350 degrees Fahrenheit). Stir every five minutes until the nuts, grains or seeds are lightly browned.

When a recipe calls for a spice ingredient to be freshly ground or freshly crushed, you can use a mortar and pestle, a rolling pin and board, or simply crush the spice with the bottom of a glass jar or mug. You may also use an electric spice grinder, which is available in most health food stores and gourmet stores.

Freshly ground spices will always have more flavor. Avoid using powdered spices that have been sitting around for months, either on store shelves or in your own kitchen.

Using Spices to Create Balance

Part of the joy of Vedic cooking is learning how to use spices to create not only different flavors but also good health. Some spices have a heating quality, while others are cooling. Some are sweet, while others are bitter or astringent. Recipes that balance Vata will naturally emphasize different spices from those that balance Pitta or Kapha.

More specifically, Vata recipes tend to favor mustard seeds, cumin, ginger, black pepper, cinnamon, cardamom, clove and salt. These spices are either gently warming or sweet.

Pitta-balancing spices include cardamom, cilantro, cinnamon, coriander, dill, fennel, mint, saffron, and small amounts of cumin and black pepper. If you are on a Pitta-balancing diet, it is important to avoid fiery-hot ingredients, such as whole chili peppers and cayenne pepper. These are much too heating for Pitta, which is already hot by nature.

Hot spices are good for balancing Kapha. Kapha recipes are generally the spiciest of all, because Kapha thrives on the heat and stimulation that comes from eating spicy food. The only spice ingredient that Kapha recipes try to limit is salt, because too much salt contributes to Kapha problems such as fluid retention and weight gain.

Some recipes in this book call for the addition of a churna. Churnas are spice mixtures from Maharishi Ayurveda Products International that contain all six tastes (sweet, sour, salty, pungent, bitter and astringent) in specific proportions to balance Vata, Pitta and Kapha. (For ordering information, see page 119.)

Using the appropriate churna is an easy way to make a dish delicious, and carries the added benefit of creating good health. The alternate spices included in many recipes can be used when you want to vary the flavors in a dish or enjoy the fresher taste that comes from spices prepared in your own kitchen.

Words of Caution

Herbs and spices contain the concentrated intelligence of nature. They are powerfully medicinal in their ability to create mind-body balance, and are important ingredients in many Vedic formulas. However, eating too much of any one herb or spice can create imbalances in the mind and body. Therefore, it's important to use them in moderation, and to use them in the right way. The recipes in this book will show you how to combine small amounts of various herbs and spices to create only nourishing, healthful effects.

Onion and garlic are featured prominently in many cuisines around the world. This is not the case in Vedic cooking, which uses only small amounts carefully combined with other ingredients. If used properly, both have great medicinal value, but a word of caution is in order. If you find that eating onion and garlic interferes with your experiences in meditation, then omit them completely from your diet and try using asafoetida (hing) instead. It's a good flavor substitute, and causes no ill effects.

Finally, many cooks think nothing of using the same spoon for stirring and tasting. In Ayurvedic cooking, this is considered very unhygienic. If you want to taste a dish before serving it, spoon a little into a separate dish and use a tasting spoon. This maintains the cleanliness of the dish. This is very important, even if you are cooking just for yourself or your family.

Staples in Ayurvedic Cuisine

Bean Soups

A freshly cooked bean soup called "dal" is a staple in Ayurvedic cuisine and helps provide the protein that vegetarians need. Every main meal will usually include dal, served with rice and vegetables. Bread, salad, chutney and dessert may be added to complete the meal.

Beans can take a long time to cook. To cut the cooking time in half, try using a pressure cooker, or let your beans cook in a crockpot overnight.

The secret to making a delicious dal is in the spicing. These recipes will acquaint you with the herbs and spices that are used most often.

Vegetables

In this section you will find a variety of vegetable curry dishes. "Curry" here does not refer to the curry powder that is available in your local grocery store. It refers to a dish that is flavored with a variety of different spices.

In India, there is no one curry powder. There are dozens of different spice mixtures, always ground fresh before use. The name curry probably comes from the fact that many curry dishes do include curry leaves, from the plant murraya koenigii. These flavorful leaves can be found in the refrigerated section of Indian or Asian grocery stores.

Vegetable curry dishes add color, taste and nutrition to a balanced Ayurvedic meal.

Grains

A freshly made grain dish is an important part of every main meal in Ayurvedic cooking. Served with dal, grains help give vegetarians a balanced and healthful diet. Favor whole grains whenever possible because they are fresher and more nutritious.

White basmati rice is the best everyday grain for balancing Vata and Pitta. Wheat is also good for balancing Vata and Pitta. Millet, barley, corn and rye are better for balancing Kapha, although rice and wheat may be taken in moderation.

Grain dishes can be extremely simple or made festive with vegetables, spices, raisins and nuts. Cook your grains on top of the stove, or experiment with a crockpot or automatic rice cooker.

Salads

In the West, eating a cold, raw salad for lunch is considered healthy. This is not the case in Maharishi Vedic Medicine because raw foods are difficult for most people to digest.

In the Vedic tradition, salads are acceptable when served at room temperature, in small amounts, and early in a meal when the digestive fire is strong. Then a salad adds freshness to the physiology. But the bulk of every main meal should be warm, well-cooked food, freshly prepared, because such food is easier to digest and provides the most nourishment.

These recipes are designed to be a side dish for two or three people.

Chutneys

India is famous for its flavorful chutneys. A chutney is a spicy condiment that complements and accents main dishes.

In Maharishi Vedic Medicine, a spoonful or two of chutney taken with a meal is considered very balancing because it provides all six tastes—sweet, sour, salty, pungent, bitter and astringent.

Breads

The recipes in this section contain little or no leavening. These "flatbreads" are the healthiest to eat because yeast and other rising agents cause imbalances that can interfere with digestion.

In India, chapati flatbreads are served with almost every meal. The flour used in chapatis is a special low-gluten flour from the whole kernel of soft-textured wheat. This kind of whole-grain bread, freshly made at home, is highly recommended in Maharishi Vedic Medicine.

In addition to wheat flour, flatbreads often contain rice or bean flours. This makes them particularly nourishing and balancing for everyone.

Desserts

In Maharishi Vedic Medicine, desserts are considered especially balancing for Vata and Pitta. Desserts that are sweetened with raw honey (rather than sugar) are balancing for Kapha. So you can feel comfortable including desserts in all your meal planning.

If the dessert is rich and heavy (such as frosted cake or cream pie), eat it first, before the rest of your food. This is because your digestive fire is strongest at the beginning of a meal. A light dessert (such as cooked fruit) can be enjoyed at the end of a meal.

It's important to remember that everything should be taken in moderation, especially sweets. Never snack on sweets between meals because this ruins digestion and creates a toxic waste in the body called *ama*.

Beverages

One of the most important guidelines in Maharishi Vedic Medicine is to avoid ice-cold food and beverages. In the West, ice water is standard at the dinner table, but this interferes with digestion because it puts out the digestive fire. So drink your beverages warm or at room temperature, but never ice-cold.

It's good to sip a beverage with your meal, but avoid large quantities of liquids immediately before or immediately after a big meal. A freshly made yogurt drink called lassi, taken with your meal, is excellent for digestion.

Basic Dairy Recipes

Milk is considered an ideal food in Maharishi Vedic Medicine. To make it more digestible, boil it for a few minutes before drinking it. Drink it warm or let it cool to room temperature, as you like.

It's important to drink milk separately from a meal containing mixed tastes. Milk is considered "sweet" by nature, so enjoy it alone or with other sweet foods such as toast, cereal, dates or almonds.

The following are recipes for basic dairy ingredients that are used by all three doshas.

Ghee

1 lb. unsalted butter

Heat butter over medium heat in a sturdy pan. Let butter melt completely. When it starts to boil, reduce the heat to low and watch carefully so that it doesn't boil over or burn. Continue boiling until the milk fat particles separate and settle to the bottom, and all the moisture evaporates.

When it is done, the ghee will have a clear golden color and a sweet aroma. The sediment at the bottom will be brown. Remove the pan from the heat and allow the ghee to cool slightly. Then carefully strain the ghee into a clean, dry glass jar, using a fine mesh strainer or cheesecloth. You may have to strain it twice to remove all the solids.

Ghee is perfect for cooking and baking, and may be used instead of butter on toast, rice, potatoes, popcorn and other dishes. In moderation, ghee is the healthiest oil to include in your daily diet.

You may also order organic ghee from Maharishi Ayurveda Products International (see page 119).

Panir (Fresh Cheese)

> 1/2 gallon whole milk
>
> juice from 1 1/2 lemons

Slowly bring milk to a boil in a heavy-bottomed pan over medium heat. When the milk rises up and comes to a steady boil, lower the heat and add the lemon juice. Stir very gently. The milk will start to curdle and form a spongy ball of cheese. Add a little more lemon juice if the milk does not begin to curdle in a minute or two.

When the milk has finished curdling, the liquid will be clear greenish yellow. Pour off this liquid whey and allow the curd to sit in a colander over a bowl to drain any excess liquid for 40 to 60 minutes. You may then use the curd immediately, or refrigerate it for use within a couple of days.

Fresh homemade cheese is much healthier and more digestible than store-bought cheeses that are aged and have unhealthy additives. Whey is also very healthy and may be used to make rice or in soups and vegetable dishes.

Yogurt

> 2 cups whole milk
>
> 2 teaspoons plain yogurt

Slowly bring milk to a boil over medium heat. Take pan off the heat and allow milk to cool down to lukewarm or body temperature. Pour milk into a glass jar and stir in plain yogurt.

Cover jar with lid and wrap a dish towel around the jar. If you have an electric oven, place the jar in the oven near the light bulb and keep the oven light on during the night. Or store the wrapped jar in a warm pantry next to a turned-on light. In the morning (approximately 6–7 hours later), you will have fresh homemade yogurt that is sweet and not acidic.

You can also use an electric yogurt maker (available in most health food stores) to make your yogurt.

Yogurt should only be used when it is freshly made.

Using the proportions in this recipe, make only enough yogurt for you and your family to eat the next day. It is not necessary to refrigerate this yogurt before you use it. It is better to eat yogurt at lunch, when it is easier to digest.

In the summer, you may find that you don't need a full teaspoon of starter yogurt per cup of milk. One-half teaspoon may be enough. On the other hand, you may need a little more starter in the winter. Using too much or too little starter will make your yogurt sour or bitter, or it may not thicken properly.

SECTION TWO

Vata-Balancing Recipes

Bean Soups

Creamy Red Lentil Dal

1/2 cup red lentils (masoor dal)
1 1/2 cups water (or more for thinner dal)
1 pinch cinnamon
1 pinch nutmeg
1/4 teaspoon turmeric
2 teaspoons ghee
1 teaspoon cumin seeds
1/4 teaspoon fresh ginger root, grated
1/2 cup butternut squash or yams
1/4 cup sour cream (optional)
1/4 teaspoon ground fenugreek
1 teaspoon ground coriander
1/2 teaspoon salt

Rinse the lentils well and add to boiling water. Cover and let simmer on low for about 30 minutes, until they start to dissolve. While simmering, add cinnamon, nutmeg and turmeric.

In a separate frying pan, sauté cumin seeds and fresh ginger in ghee. Add finely chopped squash to the spice mixture and sauté for five minutes. Then add the squash and spices to the dal along with the sour cream, fenugreek and coriander.

Simmer until squash is tender. Add salt at the end of cooking.

Serves 2 to 3.

Rice and Dal

1/4 cup white basmati rice
1/4 cup split hulled mung beans
2 cups water (or more for thinner dal)
1/2 cup carrots, sliced
1/2 cup asparagus, sliced
2 teaspoons ghee
1 tablespoon fresh ginger root, grated
2 teaspoons Vata Churna (or 1 teaspoon
    ground coriander, 1/4 teaspoon ground fenu-
    greek and 1 pinch hing)
1/2 teaspoon turmeric
1/2 teaspoon salt
1 teaspoon cilantro leaves, minced

Rinse rice and mung beans well. Boil water and add rice
and beans. Reduce heat to low and add the vegetables.

In a separate pan, sauté the fresh ginger, Vata Churna
(or alternate spices) and turmeric in ghee and add to the rice
and beans. Cook, covered, for about one hour. Stir to prevent sticking.

Add salt at the end of cooking. Garnish with cilantro
before serving.

Serves 2 to 3.

Sambar Dal

3/4 cup split hulled mung beans
2 1/4 cups water (or more for thinner dal)
1 tablespoon ghee
1/4 teaspoon black mustard seeds
1 tablespoon Vata Churna (or 1 teaspoon
    ground cumin, 1 teaspoon ground coriander,
    1/2 teaspoon ground fennel and 1 pinch
    hing)
1 teaspoon turmeric

1/4 cup dried unsweetened shredded coconut
1/8 cup carrots, sliced
1/2 cup fresh green peas (or frozen)
1/8 cup cauliflower, cut into flowerets
1/2 tomato, diced
1 teaspoon salt
1/2 teaspoon lemon juice

Rinse beans well. Add water and bring to a boil. Reduce to low heat and cover. Cook for about 30 minutes or until beans begin to dissolve.

In a separate frying pan, heat the ghee over medium heat. Add mustard seeds and fry until they start popping. Then add the Vata Churna (or alternate spices) and turmeric. Then add the coconut and fry until it is golden, stirring continuously. Add vegetables and allow the mixture to cook for about five minutes.

Add mixture to dal and cook for about 15 minutes until the vegetables are soft. Add salt at the end of cooking, and lemon juice just before serving.

Serves 2 to 3.

Split Mung Dal

3/4 cup split hulled mung beans
2 1/4 cups water (or more for thinner dal)
2 teaspoons ghee
1 teaspoon fresh ginger root, grated
1 fresh curry leaf (optional)
1 tablespoon Vata Churna (or 1/4 teaspoon
    black mustard seeds, 1/2 teaspoon coriander
    seeds, freshly crushed, and 1/4 teaspoon
    turmeric)
salt to taste
1 teaspoon lemon juice
1/2 teaspoon cilantro leaves, minced

Rinse beans well. Add water and bring to a boil. Reduce heat to low and cover for 30 minutes or until the beans start to dissolve.

In a frying pan sauté fresh ginger in ghee until lightly browned. Add the curry leaf and then the Vata Churna. (If using alternate spices, fry them in this order: black mustard seeds, fresh ginger, coriander, curry leaf, turmeric.) Add spice mixture to the mung beans with salt.

Simmer for several more minutes. Before serving add lemon juice and cilantro.

Serves 2 to 3

Split Mung Dal with Vegetables

1/2 cup split hulled mung beans
1 1/2 cups water (or more for thinner dal)
1/4 cup carrots, peeled and sliced
1 tablespoon ghee
1 teaspoon black mustard seeds
1 teaspoon cumin seeds
1 teaspoon fresh ginger root, grated
1 pinch hing
1/4 teaspoon turmeric
1 1/2 teaspoons ground coriander
1/2 cup parsnips, peeled and sliced
1/4 cup zucchini, peeled and sliced
1/2 teaspoon salt

Rinse beans well and add to boiling water. Reduce to low heat and add carrots.

In a separate frying pan, sauté mustard seeds in ghee until they pop. Add cumin seeds, fresh ginger, hing, turmeric and coriander. Then add parsnips and zucchini to the spice mixture. Let the vegetables cook for five minutes, then add mixture to the dal.

Cover and let dal simmer until the mung beans dissolve and the parsnips are very tender. Add salt at the end, before serving.

Serves 2 to 3.

Sweet Dal

3/4 cup chana dal
2 1/4 cups water (or more for thinner dal)
1 bay leaf
1 tomato, cubed
2 teaspoons butter
1 tablespoon ghee
1/4 teaspoon cumin seeds
1/2 teaspoon fresh ginger root, grated
1 pinch hing
1/8 teaspoon ground coriander
2 tablespoons fresh or dried coconut
2 tablespoons brown sugar
1 teaspoon salt

Rinse beans well and soak overnight. Drain the water the next morning and rinse beans again. Add fresh cooking water. Bring the water to a boil and add the beans and the bay leaf. Cook over medium-high heat for about 30 minutes.

Stir the beans well. Cover and reduce to a simmer. Add the tomato to the dal along with the butter. Continue simmering for another 30 minutes.

In a separate pan, heat the ghee and fry the cumin seeds, fresh ginger, hing, coriander and coconut. Fry until coconut turns golden, stirring continuously.

Add the mixture to the dal along with the sugar and salt. Continue simmering for about five minutes or until dal is done.

Serves 2 to 3.

Whole Green Mung Dal

>1/2 cup whole green mung beans
>1 1/2 cups water (or more for thinner dal)
>1 bay leaf
>1/4 teaspoon turmeric
>1/4 cup grated carrot
>1 tablespoon ghee
>1 teaspoon fresh ginger root, grated
>1/2 teaspoon fennel seeds
>1/2 teaspoon ground cumin
>1 teaspoon ground coriander
>1/4 cup tomato, chopped
>1 teaspoon salt
>1 teaspoon sugar
>1 teaspoon lemon juice
>1 tablespoon cilantro leaves, minced

Rinse the mung beans well and soak overnight. The next day drain the water, rinse beans again, and add fresh cooking water. Bring to a boil with the bay leaf, turmeric and carrots. Cook on low for 45 minutes, until beans are soft.

In a separate frying pan, sauté in ghee the fresh ginger, fennel seeds, cumin and coriander. Add tomatoes to the spice mixture. Cook for about three minutes. Add spice mixture and salt to the dal.

Before serving add sugar, lemon juice and cilantro.

Serves 2 to 3.

Vegetables

Asparagus Curry

>1 1/2 cups asparagus, cut into 1/2-inch pieces
>1 tablespoon ghee
>1 teaspoon Vata Churna (or 1/2 teaspoon

ground cumin, 1/2 teaspoon ground coriander, 1/4 teaspoon turmeric, 1 pinch ground
fenugreek and 1 pinch hing)
3 tablespoons water
1/4 teaspoon salt

Sauté Vata Churna (or alternate spices) in ghee, then
add asparagus. Stir-fry for several minutes. Add water, cover
pan, and cook over medium heat until tender. Add salt at the
end of cooking.
Serves 2.

Beet Soup

1 cup fresh beets, cut into 1/4-inch pieces
1/4 cup white potato, cut into 1/4-inch pieces
1/2 teaspoon fresh parsley, minced
1 tablespoon ghee
1/4 cup leeks (white part), finely sliced
   (optional)
2 cups water (or more)
2 tablespoons lemon juice
2 teaspoons sugar
salt and pepper to taste
2 tablespoons yogurt

Sauté leeks in ghee for five minutes in a deep pot. Add
water, beets, potato and parsley. Bring to a boil, then cover
pot and reduce heat to medium low. Allow to cook for about
45 minutes until beets and potatoes are tender.
   Add lemon juice, sugar, salt and pepper. Stir well. Serve
with a dollop of yogurt on top.
   Serves 2 to 3.

Butternut Squash Curry

> 1 1/2 cups butternut squash, yams, or sweet
>   potatoes
> 1 tablespoon ghee
> 2 teaspoons Vata Churna (or 1 teaspoon
>   coriander seeds, freshly ground, 1/4 tea-
>   spoon ground cumin and 1 pinch ground
>   fenugreek)
> 2 teaspoons cashews, chopped
> 1 teaspoon brown sugar
> 1 tablespoon raisins
> 1/2 teaspoon salt
> 1/4 cup cilantro leaves, minced

Bake or steam squash, then cube or mash and set aside.

In a separate pan, sauté Vata Churna (or alternate spices) in ghee. Add cashews, brown sugar and raisins.

Add the cooked squash to the spice mixture. Add salt and cilantro. Cook for another five minutes.

Serves 2.

Creamy Asparagus

> 2 cups asparagus, cut into 1/2-inch pieces
> 1 pinch saffron threads
> 1 tablespoon ghee
> 1 tablespoon flour
> 1/2 cup cream

Steam asparagus until tender, with saffron added to the water. Save 1/2 cup asparagus water.

Heat the ghee, then add flour, stirring constantly. Cook the mixture for a couple of minutes, then add the asparagus water and the cream. Cook to a thick sauce consistency. Add the cooked asparagus to the cream sauce. Heat for several more minutes, then serve over rice.

Serves 2 to 3.

Gingered Carrots

> 2 cups carrots, quartered and cut into inch-long
> sticks
> 1 tablespoon unsalted butter or ghee
> 2 tablespoons fresh ginger root, grated
> 1/4 teaspoon Vata Churna
> 2 tablespoons brown sugar

Partially cook carrots by boiling them in water for about three minutes. Remove from the heat and set aside.

In a separate frying pan heat butter or ghee and add fresh ginger, Vata Churna and brown sugar and cook for a couple of minutes. Add the drained carrots to the spices and continue to cook for another five minutes, until the carrots are tender.

Serves 2 to 3.

Mixed Vegetable Curry

> 1/2 cup green beans
> 1/2 cup tomato
> 1/4 cup sweet potato
> 1/4 cup zucchini
> 1/8 cup carrots
> 2 tablespoons ghee
> 2 teaspoons fresh ginger root, grated
> 2 teaspoons Vata Churna
> water
> salt to taste
> 2 teaspoons cilantro leaves, minced
> 1 teaspoon lemon juice

Cut or dice vegetables into pieces and set aside. Sauté fresh ginger in ghee. Add Vata Churna. Add cut vegetables to the spice mixture and stir. Add several tablespoons of

water and cover pan. Let vegetables cook until they are tender. Add salt, cilantro and lemon juice during the last five minutes of cooking.
Serves 2.

Panir and Green Beans

1 cup panir, cubed (see recipe on page 31)
1 cup green beans, cut into 1/2-inch pieces
1 tablespoon ghee
1/2 teaspoon black mustard seeds
1/4 cup cashews, chopped
1 teaspoon Vata Churna
1/2 teaspoon ground cumin
1/2 cup tomato, diced
salt to taste

Steam green beans until almost done.
In a separate pan, pop mustard seeds in hot ghee. Add cashews and lightly roast. Add Vata Churna and cumin. Then add panir and lightly fry for about five minutes. Add steamed green beans and tomato and cook with cover on for another five minutes. You may need to add some water if it becomes too dry. Add salt at the end of cooking.
Serves 2 to 3.

Panir and Pumpkin Curry

3/4 cup panir, cut into 1/2-inch pieces (see recipe on page 31)
1 1/2 cups fresh pumpkin
2 threads saffron, crumbled
1/4 cup hot water
2 teaspoons ghee
1 teaspoon fresh ginger root, grated
1/2 teaspoon ground cumin

1 teaspoon ground coriander
1 teaspoon brown sugar
1/2 cup tomato, chopped (optional)
1 pinch nutmeg
salt to taste
1/2 cup sour cream

Steam or bake pumpkin until barely tender. Then scoop it out of its shell, mash and set aside. Soak saffron in hot water for 20 minutes.

In a separate pan, sauté fresh ginger in ghee, then add cumin, coriander and brown sugar. Add the panir and cooked pumpkin to the spice mixture and sauté for several minutes. Add tomato, saffron water and nutmeg and cook for about 15 minutes over medium heat. Add salt and sour cream and cook for a few more minutes before serving.

Serves 2 to 3.

Tofu Vegetable Stir-Fry

1/2 cup firm tofu, cut into 1/2-inch chunks
1 cup tomato, diced
1/2 cup carrots, finely sliced
1/4 cup spinach or kale, chopped
1/8 cup mung bean sprouts
1 tablespoon toasted sesame oil (the kind that is
    used in Chinese cooking)
1 teaspoon sesame seeds
1 teaspoon fresh ginger root, grated
1 teaspoon Vata Churna salt and pepper to
    taste
1 teaspoon cilantro leaves, minced
1/2 teaspoon lemon juice (optional)

Heat sesame oil over medium heat. Add sesame seeds and lightly brown. Watch closely because they burn easily.

Add fresh ginger and sauté briefly. Add tofu and sauté for several minutes. Add vegetables and Vata Churna. Cover and cook until vegetables are tender.

Add salt and pepper to taste. Garnish with cilantro and lemon juice before serving.

Serves 2 to 3.

Zucchini and Tomato Curry

  2 zucchinis, peeled and cut into 1/2-inch pieces
  2 tomatoes, quartered
  1 tablespoon ghee
  1 teaspoon cumin seed
  1 teaspoon fresh ginger root, grated
  1 pinch hing
  1/4 teaspoon turmeric
  1/2 teaspoon ground coriander
  1/2 teaspoon lemon juice
  salt to taste
  1 teaspoon cilantro leaves, minced

Heat ghee and sauté cumin seeds. Then add fresh ginger, hing, turmeric and coriander. Add the zucchini and stir to coat with spices. Sauté for five minutes.

Add tomatoes and lemon juice. Cover and allow to cook until tender. Add salt at the end of cooking, and cilantro just before serving.

Serves 2 to 3.

Grains

Basmati Rice

  3/4 cup white basmati rice
  1 1/2 cups water
  1/4 teaspoon salt
  2 teaspoons ghee (optional)

Rinse rice several times until water is clear. In a separate pot bring fresh water to a boil and add rice. Reduce heat to low. Cover pot and allow to simmer for 20 minutes. Add salt at the end of cooking.

When rice is done, remove from heat and lightly fluff with a fork. Add ghee and serve.

Option: For saffron rice, add three threads of crumbled saffron to water as it is boiling.

Serves 2 to 3.

Couscous Salad

3/4 cup couscous

1 cup water

1/4 cup carrots, grated and steamed
    until tender

1 tablespoon red bell pepper, minced
    and steamed until tender

1 tablespoon fresh parsley, minced

1 tablespoon pine nuts, dry-roasted

1/4 cup fresh orange juice

1 tablespoon olive oil

salt and pepper to taste

Preheat a pan on the stove. Then add couscous and stir continuously, allowing the grain to lightly toast until it turns slightly darker in color. Then add water and bring to a boil. Cover pan and remove from the heat. Let it stand for about ten minutes.

Put couscous into a serving bowl and stir in the rest of the ingredients.

Serves 2 to 3.

Flavorful Rice

> 2/3 cup white basmati rice
> 1 teaspoon ghee
> 1/2 teaspoon black mustard seeds
> 1/2 teaspoon cumin seeds
> 1 small tomato, diced
> 1/2 teaspoon turmeric
> 1 1/2 cups water
> 1/4 teaspoon salt
> 1 teaspoon lemon juice

> Rinse rice well, then spread out on a paper towel to dry.
> Pop mustard seeds in hot ghee. Add cumin seeds and
> then the tomato. Fry for one minute. Add the rice and
> turmeric. Sauté for several minutes and then add water.
> Bring water to a boil. Reduce heat to low and cover. Simmer
> for 15 or 20 minutes.
> Add salt at the end of cooking. Sprinkle with lemon juice
> before serving.
> Serves 2 to 3.

Lemon Rice

> 3/4 cup white basmati rice
> 1 1/2 cups water
> 4-5 whole cloves
> 2 teaspoons ghee
> 1 teaspoon black mustard seeds
> 1/4 teaspoon Vata Churna
> 1/2 cup lemon juice
> 1/4 teaspoon turmeric
> 1/4 teaspoon salt

> Rinse rice thoroughly and add to boiling water with
> cloves. Cover and simmer on low for 20 minutes.

In a separate pan, pop mustard seeds in hot ghee. Add Vata Churna. Remove from the heat. Let the spice mixture cool off and then add lemon juice and turmeric.

When rice is finished cooking, add the spices and salt and mix well.

Serves 2 to 3.

Rice Pilaf

1/2 cup white basmati rice
1 cup water
1/2 teaspoon turmeric
1/2 teaspoon ground cumin
2 teaspoons ghee
1/2 teaspoon fresh ginger root, grated
2 tablespoons cashews
1 tablespoon raisins
1/2 cup yogurt
1/4 teaspoon cinnamon
1/4 teaspoon salt

Rinse rice well and add to boiling water with turmeric and cumin. Cover and simmer for 20 minutes.

In a separate pan, sauté fresh ginger, cashews and raisins in ghee and add to the cooked rice.

Remove rice from the heat and add yogurt, cinnamon and salt. Mix well before serving.

Serves 2 to 3.

Vegetable Rice

3/4 cup white basmati rice
1 1/2 cups water
2-3 bay leaves
2 pinches black pepper
1 tablespoon ghee
1 teaspoon coriander seeds, freshly crushed

1/4 teaspoon turmeric
2 pinches hing
1/4 cup green beans, cut into 1/2-inch pieces
1/4 cup zucchini, cut into 1/4-inch slices
1/4 cup parsnips, cut into 1/4-inch slices
1 tablespoon red bell pepper, minced
1/4 teaspoon salt
1 tablespoon blanched almonds, dry-roasted

Rinse rice well. Bring water to a boil, then add rice, bay leaves and pepper. Reduce heat to low, cover, and let simmer for 20 minutes.

In a separate pan, fry the remaining spices in ghee and then add vegetables. Cook until tender. Add salt at the end of cooking.

When rice and vegetables are done cooking, combine them on a serving dish and stir lightly. Garnish with almonds.

Serves 3.

Wheat Berry Salad

1/2 cup wheat berries
2 cups water
1/2 cup fresh peaches, diced
2 tablespoons dried cranberries
2 tablespoons pine nuts, dry-roasted
1 tablespoon cilantro leaves, minced
1/4 teaspoon hing
1/4 teaspoon ground cumin
salt and pepper to taste
2 tablespoons olive oil
2 tablespoons lemon juice

Rinse the wheat berries thoroughly. Bring water to a boil and add wheat berries. Cover and reduce heat to low. Cook for about 45 minutes until berries are tender but of a chewy consistency.

Remove from the heat and allow to cool to room temperature. Add the rest of the ingredients and toss with olive oil and lemon juice.

Serves 2 to 3.

Salads

Carrot Beet Salad

1/2 cup carrots, grated
1/2 cup beets, grated
1 tablespoon capers
1 teaspoon lemon juice
1 tablespoon olive oil
salt and pepper to taste

Mix ingredients well and serve.
Serves 2 to 3.

Cucumber Salad

1 cucumber, peeled and diced
2 tablespoons olive oil
1/2 teaspoon black mustard seeds
1/4 teaspoon cumin seeds
1/2 tomato, chopped
2 tablespoons cashews, dry-roasted and
    coarsely chopped
1 tablespoon cilantro leaves, minced
a few pinches turmeric
1 teaspoon lemon juice
1/4 teaspoon sugar
1/4 teaspoon salt

Pop mustard seeds in hot olive oil. Add cumin seeds and tomato and sauté for three minutes.

Add mixture to the cucumbers. Add cashews, cilantro,

turmeric, lemon juice mixed with sugar, and salt. Stir well
and serve.
Serves 2 to 3.

Grated Vegetable Salad

    1 tablespoon mung bean sprouts
    1 tablespoon carrots, finely shredded
    1 tablespoon beets, shredded
    1 tablespoon daikon root, shredded
    1 tablespoon cilantro leaves, chopped
    1 teaspoon fresh basil, minced
    1 teaspoon fresh ginger root, grated
    1 teaspoon sesame seeds, dry-roasted
    1 tablespoon olive or sesame oil
    1/4 teaspoon ground cumin
    black salt or table salt to taste
    1 tablespoon lime juice
    one teaspoon sugar (optional)

    Toss ingredients together and mix well. (If you use
sugar, mix it with the lime juice before adding to the salad.)
Serves 2 to 3.

Panir Salad

    1 cup panir, cubed (see recipe on page 31)
    1/4 cup artichoke hearts, sliced
    1/4 cup carrots, sliced and steamed
    1 tablespoon cilantro leaves, minced
    1 tablespoon lemon juice
    3 tablespoons yogurt
    1/2 teaspoon cumin seeds, dry-roasted
    1/8 teaspoon hing
    1/4 teaspoon salt

    Prepare the dressing by combining lemon juice, yogurt,

cumin, hing and salt. Add panir, artichoke hearts, steamed carrots and cilantro. Mix well and serve.

Serves 2 to 3.

Pasta Salad

2 cups corkscrew pasta
1/4 cup yogurt
1 tablespoon lemon juice
1 tablespoon olive oil
1/4 teaspoon dried basil
2 pinches hing
salt and pepper to taste
1/2 cup avocado, cut into small chunks
1 tablespoon Greek black olives, pitted
1 teaspoon pine nuts, dry-roasted

Cook the pasta and set aside.

In a separate bowl, mix yogurt, lemon juice, olive oil, basil, hing, salt and pepper. Then add avocado, olives, pine nuts and cooked pasta. Mix well and serve.

Serves 2 to 3.

Chutneys

Avocado Chutney

1 ripe avocado, mashed
1 tomato, cut into small pieces
2 teaspoons ghee
1/2 teaspoon ground cumin
1/4 teaspoon hing
1/2 teaspoon ground coriander
1 tablespoon lemon juice
1/2 teaspoon sugar
1/4 teaspoon salt
1/4 teaspoon black pepper

Sauté cumin, hing and coriander in ghee. Add the tomato and sauté for about five minutes. You may need to add a tablespoon of water if the tomato sticks to the pan.

Allow mixture to cool, then add avocado and lemon juice. Add sugar, salt and pepper and serve.

Serves 2 to 3.

Fresh Mango Chutney

1 ripe mango
1 teaspoon ghee
1/2 teaspoon black mustard seeds
1 tablespoon fresh ginger root, grated
1 tablespoon lime juice
1/4 teaspoon cinnamon
2 pinches hing

Sauté black mustard seeds in ghee until they pop. Remove from the heat.

Mix all the ingredients in a blender or food processor until they form a thick purée.

Serves 2 to 3.

Mint Coconut Chutney

1/2 cup fresh mint leaves
1/4 cup fresh coconut, grated (or dried
    unsweetened shredded coconut)
2 teaspoons ghee
1 tablespoon fresh ginger root, grated
a few pinches hing
1/2 cup yogurt
1 tablespoon sugar
1/4 teaspoon salt
1 pinch black pepper

Sauté fresh ginger and hing in ghee. Add coconut and sauté until golden, stirring continuously.

Put mixture in a blender or food processor with the mint leaves, yogurt, sugar, salt and pepper. Blend until it forms a thick paste.

Serves 2 to 3.

Pineapple Chutney

1 cup fresh pineapple, cubed
1 1/2 teaspoons ghee
1/2 teaspoon cumin seeds
1/4 teaspoon turmeric
1/4 teaspoon cinnamon
2 tablespoons sugar (or to taste)
salt to taste

Sauté cumin seeds in ghee. Then blend all ingredients in a blender or food processor until they form a thick, smooth texture.

Serves 2 to 3.

Raisin Cilantro Chutney

1/2 cup raisins, soaked for two hours
3/4 cup cilantro leaves
2 tablespoons fresh ginger root, grated
1/2 teaspoon lemon rind, finely grated
1/2 teaspoon poppy seeds, dry-roasted
2 tablespoons lemon juice
1/4 teaspoon salt
black pepper to taste

Blend ingredients in a blender or food processor until they form a thick paste.

Serves 2 to 3.

Breads

Chapati Flatbread

> 1 cup chapati flour or whole wheat pastry flour
> 1/2 teaspoon salt
> 1 teaspoon oil
> 1/2 cup warm water
> ghee
>
> For this recipe you will need a wooden rolling pin, a wooden or marble cutting board, tongs and a wire cake cooler.
>
> *Dough instructions:*
> Mix flour, salt, oil and water, pouring in water a little at a time while stirring with a fork. Knead for five to seven minutes until the dough is soft and smooth. (It should be the texture of a fresh jar of children's Play-Doh.) Allow dough to sit for 20 to 30 minutes in a bowl with a damp paper towel or cloth over it. Knead for another two minutes and then make into 3/4-inch balls. Roll each ball into a circle approximately five inches in diameter and 1/4 inch thick.
>
> *Cooking instructions:*
> Use the two front burners on your stove to cook the chapatis. Place an iron skillet over medium-high heat on one burner. The other burner should be turned to low. If you have an electric stove, place a wire cake cooler over the second burner.
> Heat 1/4 teaspoon ghee in the skillet and spread it around evenly with a paper towel. Place one of the uncooked chapatis in the skillet and cook for several minutes until the dough bubbles or blisters. Then turn the chapati over and cook for several more minutes until light brown spots cover both sides.
> Pick up the chapati with tongs and place it on top of the

other burner. If you have a gas stove, it should not touch the fire directly, but rest on the burner above the flame. If you have an electric stove, place the chapati on the wire cake cooler above the electric burner. The bread should puff up within seconds. Turn the bread over and let the other side puff up. Spread ghee over the bread and serve right away.

If you find it difficult to cook chapatis using this traditional method, try using an electric tortilla maker. The texture and taste of the bread will change, but it will still be healthy and wholesome.

This recipe makes about five chapatis.

Dosas

1/2 cup urad dal flour
1/2 cup rice flour
1/2 teaspoon salt
1 pinch baking powder
1/2 cup water
ghee

Mix flours, salt, baking powder and water to make a smooth pancake batter. Do not over mix. You may need to add more water or more flour, depending on the thickness of the batter. Set the batter aside in a bowl for about 45 minutes.

Put a non-stick skillet on medium-high heat. Take a paper towel and spread a little ghee into the skillet. Pour about three tablespoons of batter into the pan and use the back of the spoon to spread it in a large circle, as thin as possible. Dribble small amounts of ghee around the outside of the pancake. When the pancake has developed bubbles, take a spatula and flip it over to cook the other side for several more minutes. Serve with dal, vegetables and chutney.

This recipe makes about eight dosas.

Vegetable Pancakes

3/4 cup chickpea flour
1/4 cup wheat flour
2 teaspoons Vata Churna
1/2 teaspoon salt
1/2 cup water (or more as needed)
1/2 tomato, diced
2 tablespoons carrots, grated
2 tablespoons mung bean sprouts
1 teaspoon fresh ginger root, grated
1 teaspoon cilantro leaves, minced
ghee

Mix flours, Vata Churna, salt and water to make a smooth pancake batter. Add tomato, carrots, sprouts, fresh ginger and cilantro.

Heat ghee in a large skillet and pour about two tablespoons of batter into the skillet to form each pancake. Use a spoon to spread the batter evenly. Fry each side for about five minutes over medium-high heat until golden. Serve with chutney.

This recipe makes about four pancakes.

Desserts

Apple and Rhubarb Cobbler

Filling:
2 cups rhubarb, diced
1 cup apples, peeled and diced
1/4 cup apple juice
1/4 cup sugar
1 tablespoon raisins
1 pinch nutmeg

Topping:
1/2 cup flour
1/4 cup instant oatmeal
1/2 cup brown sugar
1/4 cup cold butter, cut into small pieces

Preheat your oven to 350 degrees Fahrenheit.

Combine all the filling ingredients in a saucepan and cook with the cover on for about five minutes or until the fruit is slightly tender. Spread the mixture into a small square baking pan.

Mix the topping ingredients together until they are crumbly in texture. Sprinkle over apple-rhubarb mixture and bake for about 30 minutes, until apples are tender and the topping is lightly browned. Serve warm or at room temperature.

Serves 3 to 4.

Carrot Pudding

1 cup carrots, grated
1/4 cup blanched almonds, chopped
1/4 cup raisins
1/2 teaspoon cardamom seeds, freshly ground
1 pinch dried ginger powder
1/2 cup water (or more if necessary)
1/4 cup Almond Energy Drink or sugar
1/2 cup cream

Bring water to a boil. Add carrots, almonds, raisins, cardamom and ginger. Cover and reduce heat to low. Cook for about 20 minutes until carrots are very tender.

Add Almond Energy Drink (or sugar) and cream. Mix well. Cook until cream thickens, about 15 minutes.

Serves 2 to 3.

Date Nut Balls

    3/4 cup dried dates, cut into pieces
    3/4 cup dried figs, cut into pieces
    1/2 cup raisins
    1/2 cup sugar
    2 pinches nutmeg
    2 pinches clove
    1 pinch cinnamon
    2 cups water
    3/4 cup cashews, dry-roasted and chopped
    1/2 cup blanched almonds, chopped

Boil all the ingredients together, except for the cashews and almonds. Reduce heat and simmer for about 20 minutes, until the fruit is soft and water is almost gone.

Remove from the heat and stir in the nuts. Allow the mixture to cool until it can be handled comfortably, and then form into balls.

Serves 3 to 4.

Fruit Salad

    1 ripe mango, sliced
    1 cup cherries, pitted
    1/2 cup fresh pineapple, cut into chunks
    1/2 cup papaya, cut into chunks
    2 teaspoons raw honey
    1 teaspoon sugar
    1-2 pinches nutmeg
    1/4 cup fresh orange juice

Prepare a dressing by mixing the honey, sugar and nutmeg with the orange juice. Add to the fruit and mix well.

Serves 2 to 3.

Rice Pudding

> 1/4 cup white basmati rice
> 1 tablespoon raisins (optional)
> 1 cup water
> 1 cup milk
> 1/4 cup Almond Energy Drink or sugar
> 1/4 teaspoon ground cardamom
> 1/4 cup cream
> 1 teaspoon rose water or to taste

Rinse rice well. Bring the water to a boil. Cook rice and raisins in the water for 20 minutes. Rice will be mushy.

Add milk and bring to a boil. Lower heat to a simmer and add Almond Energy Drink (or sugar), cardamom and cream. Allow to cook for about an hour and a half, stirring occasionally, until you have a thick pudding.

Allow to cool and then add rose water.

Serves 2 to 3.

Tapioca Pudding

> 1/2 cup tapioca pearls
> 1 1/2 cups milk
> 1/4 cup sugar
> 3 threads saffron
> 1 pinch ground cardamom
> 1/2 teaspoon rose water (optional)

Soak tapioca overnight in two cups of water. The next day drain the water.

Bring milk, tapioca, sugar, saffron and cardamom to a boil. Reduce heat to the lowest possible simmer and cover. (You may want to use a double boiler to prevent burning.)

Simmer for about one hour until pearls are tender and liquid has evaporated. Stir occasionally to prevent sticking. Remove from the heat and allow to cool to room temperature. Sprinkle with rose water.

Serves 2 to 3.

Beverages

Digestive Lassi

>1/4 cup yogurt
>3/4 cup water
>1 pinch dried ginger powder
>1 pinch ground cumin
>1 pinch ground coriander
>1 pinch clove or black pepper
>1 pinch rock salt or black salt

Blend all ingredients in a blender and serve. This drink is especially good for digestion.

Options:
Vary the spices in different ways. For a simple lassi, add only cumin, coriander and black salt.
Serves 1.

Mint Lassi

>1 small bunch of fresh mint leaves
>1 cup water
>1/2 cup yogurt
>2 tablespoons sugar or to taste
>2 tablespoons cream (optional)

Remove the thicker stems from the mint leaves. Purée leaves with the water. Add the rest of the ingredients and blend until smooth.
Serves 1 to 2.

Rose Lassi

>1/2 cup yogurt
>1 cup water
>1 tablespoon Rose Petal Conserve or to taste
>   (or 1 teaspoon rose water plus 1 tablespoon
>   sugar)
>2 tablespoons cream (optional)

Blend ingredients until smooth. This makes a very cooling, refreshing drink in the summer.
Serves 1 to 2.

Royal Mango Lassi

1/2 cup yogurt
1 1/4 cups water
1/2 cup fresh mango
2 tablespoons sugar or to taste
1/2 teaspoon ground cardamom
2 tablespoons cream (optional)

Blend all ingredients in a blender until smooth.
Serves 2.

Warm Milk and Ginger

1 cup milk
1/2 teaspoon fresh ginger root, grated
1 teaspoon sugar or raw honey

Slowly bring milk to a boil with the fresh ginger. Gently boil for a few minutes. Remove from the heat and cool to drinking temperature. Add sugar or honey to taste. This is a good drink to have about a half hour before going to bed.

Options:
For breakfast try adding Almond Energy Drink instead of sugar or honey.
For a gentle laxative effect, add a little melted ghee (one-half teaspoon or one teaspoon) to the milk and drink it when it is still very warm.
Serves 1.

Menu Suggestions

It is best to eat three meals a day. According to Maharishi Vedic Medicine, breakfast should be the lightest meal of the day.

Your main meal should be lunch because your digestive fire is strongest in the middle of the day. Eat lunch sometime between 11:30 and 1:30 and at the same time each day. The suggestions given in this section for lunch are ideal, but if you don't have time to prepare so many dishes, give yourself at least one substantial hot dish, supplemented with salad, bread and fruit.

Dinner should be lighter than lunch. Eat your dinner early in the evening for best digestion. The later you eat, the lighter your meal should be.

Breakfast

Toast with Cashew Delight and Rose Petal
   Conserve
Warm Milk and Ginger (see page 63)
Stewed apples or pears cooked with cloves
Cream of wheat cereal
Vata Tea
Cooked oatmeal
Dates stuffed with a small amount of ghee
Vata Tea
Rice Pudding (see page 61)
Raja's Cup
Chapati Flatbread (see page 56)
Warm Milk with Almond Energy Drink (see
   page 63)

Lunch

Split Mung Dal (see page 37)
Asparagus Curry (see page 40)
Basmati Rice (see page 46)
Carrot Beet Salad (see page 51)
Raisin Cilantro Chutney (see page 55)
Chapati Flatbread (see page 56)
Rose Lassi (see page 62)
Creamy Red Lentil Dal (see page 35)
Mixed Vegetable Curry (see page 43)
Rice Pilaf (see page 49)   ˙
Pineapple Chutney (see page 55)
Mint Lassi (see page 62)
Whole Green Mung Dal (see page 40)
Butternut Squash Curry (see page 42)
Lemon Rice (see page 48)
Grated Vegetable Salad (see page 52)
Fruit Salad (see page 60)

Dinner

Split Mung Dal (see page 37)
Vegetable Rice (see page 49)
Chapati Flatbread (see page 56)
Split Mung Dal with Vegetables (see page 38)
Tapioca Pudding (see page 61)
Sambar Dal (see page 36)
Dosas (see page 57)
Rice and Dal (see page 36)
Vegetable Pancakes (see page 58)

SECTION THREE

Pitta-Balancing Recipes

Bean Soups

Brown Lentil Dal

> 3/4 cup brown lentils
> 2 1/4 cups water (or more for thinner dal)
> 1/4 cup sweet potatoes, steamed
> 1 teaspoon ground coriander
> 1/2 teaspoon ground cumin
> 1/2 teaspoon turmeric
> 1 pinch fennel seeds
> 1 tablespoon ghee
> 2 tablespoons sour cream (optional)
> salt and pepper to taste

Rinse lentils well and add to boiling water. Reduce heat to medium low for about 30 minutes. While dal is cooking, add steamed sweet potato, spices and ghee.

When the lentils are done, allow to cool slightly. Pour the dal into a blender with sour cream and blend for about 25 seconds. Add salt and pepper to taste.

Serves 2 to 3.

Garbanzo Bean Dal

> 3/4 cup garbanzo beans (also called chickpeas)
> 3 cups water
> 1/2 teaspoon turmeric
> 1/2 bay leaf
> 2 tablespoons ghee
> 1/2 teaspoon cumin seeds
> 1/2 teaspoon Pitta Churna
> 1/2 teaspoon ground coriander

2 tablespoons dried unsweetened shredded
   coconut
2 tablespoons cilantro leaves, minced
salt to taste

Rinse beans well and soak overnight. Drain the next day
and rinse again. Boil in fresh water with the turmeric and
bay leaf. Reduce heat to medium low, cover and cook for
about 45 minutes or until beans are tender.

Remove pot from the stove and drain the beans using a
colander. Set beans aside.

In a frying pan, heat the ghee and sauté in the following
order: cumin seeds, Pitta Churna, coriander, coconut. Sauté
the coconut until golden, stirring continuously. Then add the
drained beans, cilantro and salt. Sauté for several more minutes.

Serves 2 to 3.

Kidney Bean Stew

3/4 cup kidney beans
2 1/4 cups water (or more for thinner stew)
1/2 cup potato, diced
1/4 cup eggplant, diced
2 pinches turmeric
1/2 teaspoon cumin seeds, dry-roasted
1/8 cup tomato, chopped
2 tablespoons cilantro leaves, minced
1/2 teaspoon Pitta Churna (or 1/2 teaspoon
   ground coriander)
salt to taste

Rinse beans well and soak overnight. The next day drain
water and rinse again. Boil fresh water and add beans. Cook
for several minutes.

Reduce heat to medium low and continue to cook for
another 20 minutes. Then add potato, eggplant and turmeic.

Dry-roast cumin seeds and add them to the beans.

When the beans and vegetables are almost done, add tomato, cilantro and Pitta Churna (or coriander). Continue to cook for another 15 minutes. Add salt at the end of cooking.

Serves 2 to 3.

Mixed Bean Soup

1/4 cup kidney beans
1/4 cup pinto beans
1/8 cup chickpeas
2 1/4 cups water (or more for thinner soup)
1 bay leaf
1/2 teaspoon turmeric
1 tablespoon ghee
1 teaspoon cumin seeds
2 teaspoons fresh ginger root, minced
1 teaspoon ground coriander
1/2 teaspoon cardamom seeds, freshly crushed
1 tablespoon dried unsweetened shredded
    coconut
1 cup tomato, chopped
1/2 cup eggplant, cubed
1/2 cup spinach or green chard, chopped
1/2 teaspoon lime juice
1/2 teaspoon sugar
1 teaspoon salt
1 teaspoon cilantro leaves, minced

Rinse beans and chickpeas well and soak overnight. The next day drain them in a colander and rinse again. Put fresh water in a soup pot and boil. Add beans, chickpeas, bay leaf and turmeric. Lower the heat and allow beans to cook on a soft boil, covered, until the beans are tender.

While they are cooking, take a separate pan and heat the

ghee. Sauté cumin seeds until they begin to brown. Lower the heat and add fresh ginger. Then add coriander, cardamom and coconut. Cook until the coconut turns golden, stirring continuously. Add tomato and eggplant and cook for about five minutes. Then add the spinach or chard.

Cook until greens are wilted and then add the mixture to the soup. Add lime juice and sugar. Stir and simmer the soup for a few more minutes. Add salt to taste. Garnish with cilantro before serving.

Serves 2 to 3.

Rice and Dal (See recipe in Section Two, page 36)

Sambar Dal (See recipe in Section Two, page 36)

Spinach Mung Dal

> 1/2 cup split hulled mung beans
> 1 1/2 cups water (or more for thinner dal)
> 1/4 cup celery, finely chopped
> 1 tablespoon ghee
> 1 teaspoon cumin seeds
> 1/2 teaspoon fennel seeds
> 1 teaspoon ground coriander
> 1/2 teaspoon ground cardamom
> 1/2 teaspoon turmeric
> 1 cup fresh spinach, chopped
> 1 teaspoon cilantro leaves, chopped
> 1 teaspoon lime juice
> 1/2 teaspoon sugar
> 1/2 teaspoon salt

Rinse beans well. Bring water to a boil and add beans and celery. Lower heat and cover pot. Cook until beans start to dissolve.

Heat ghee over medium-high heat in a large frying pan. Sauté the cumin seeds first, then lower heat and add fennel seeds, coriander, cardamom and turmeric and cook for a few seconds. Add spinach and cook for several minutes until it is wilted.

Add mixture to the dal. Add cilantro, lime juice, sugar and salt. Stir and simmer for about five minutes.

Option: At the end, put the dal into a blender and blend until smooth.

Serves 2 to 3.

Split Mung Dal (See recipe in Section Two, page 37)

Sweet Dal (See recipe in Section Two, page 39)

Vegetables

Cooling Cucumber Soup

1 large cucumber, peeled
3 cups water
3/4 cup yogurt
1 teaspoon cumin seeds, freshly ground
black salt or table salt to taste
1 pinch black pepper
1 teaspoon cilantro leaves, minced

Slice one quarter of the cucumber into thin rounds. Set aside.

Purée the rest of the cucumber in a blender with the water. Pour cucumber purée into a saucepan and bring to a boil. Then reduce heat to a simmer for two or three minutes. Remove from the heat and cool slightly.

Put mixture back into the blender and add yogurt,

cumin, salt and pepper. Blend for two or three seconds and serve warm or at room temperature. Garnish with your saved cucumber slices and the cilantro.

Serves 2 to 3.

Cream of Spinach Curry

> 1 lb. fresh spinach, chopped and steamed
> 2 teaspoons ghee
> 1/2 teaspoon cumin seeds
> 3 tablespoons sour cream
> 1 teaspoon fresh mint leaves, minced
> salt to taste

Blend steamed spinach in a blender for several seconds and set aside.

Sauté cumin seeds in ghee and add spinach. Add sour cream, mint and salt. Cook for a few minutes, stirring gently.

Serves 2 to 3.

Fresh Fennel and Potato Curry

> 1 large fennel bulb, cut into 1/2-inch cubes
> 1 large red potato, diced
> 1 cup kale, chopped
> 2 tablespoons ghee
> 2 teaspoons Pitta Churna (or 1 teaspoon ground cumin, 1/2 teaspoon ground coriander, 1/4 teaspoon dried ginger powder and 1/4 teaspoon turmeric)
> 1/2 cup water
> 1/2 tomato, chopped
> 1 tablespoon fresh fennel greens, minced
> salt and pepper to taste

Melt ghee in a frying pan over medium-high heat. Sauté Pitta Churna (or alternate spices). Add the vegetables, except for the tomato. Stir-fry for about five minutes.

Lower the heat and add water. Cover pan and cook for about 15 minutes or until the vegetables are soft.

Stir in the tomato, fennel greens, salt and pepper and simmer for about five more minutes.

Serves 2 to 3.

Fresh Pea and Panir Curry

> 1 1/2 cups fresh snow peas
> 1 tablespoon ghee
> 1/4 teaspoon Pitta Churna
> 1/2 teaspoon ground cumin
> 1/4 teaspoon coriander seeds, freshly ground
> 3/4 cup panir, cut into small cubes (see recipe on page 31)
> 1 tablespoon cilantro leaves, chopped
> salt to taste

Lightly steam peas and set aside.

In a frying pan, heat ghee and briefly sauté Pitta Churna, cumin and coriander. Add the panir and sauté lightly. Add the steamed peas and cilantro and heat for a few minutes. Add salt to taste.

Serves 2 to 3.

Green Bean and Chickpea Stew

> 3/4 cup chickpeas, rinsed well and soaked overnight
> 3 cups water
> 1 tablespoon ghee
> 1 teaspoon Pitta Churna
> 1/4 teaspoon ground cumin
> 2 tablespoons fresh or dried coconut
> 3/4 cup green beans, cut into pieces and steamed
> 1/2 cup potato, diced and steamed
> 1/4 teaspoon turmeric
> salt to taste

2 tablespoons sour cream (optional)

1 teaspoon cilantro leaves, chopped

Drain the chickpeas, rinse again, then cook in fresh water until tender. Drain and set aside.

Sauté Pitta Churna, cumin and coconut in ghee, stirring continuously. When coconut turns golden, add steamed green beans, steamed potato and cooked chickpeas, and sauté for several minutes.

Add turmeric, salt and sour cream. Continue cooking for five more minutes. Garnish with cilantro.

Serves 3.

Green Beans and Coconut

2 cups green beans, cut into 1/2-inch pieces

1 tablespoon ghee

1/2 teaspoon fresh ginger root, grated

2 1/2 tablespoons fresh coconut, grated (or dried unsweetened shredded coconut)

1/4 cup coconut milk*

1/4 teaspoon ground cardamom

salt to taste

1 pinch black pepper

Steam the green beans lightly and set aside.

In a separate pan, sauté the fresh ginger in ghee. Then add two tablespoons of the coconut, stirring continuously. Add the steamed green beans and sauté for three minutes.

Add the coconut milk and cardamom. Cover pan and simmer for five minutes until the green beans are tender. Add salt and pepper and stir. Garnish with the rest of the coconut.

Serves 2 to 3.

---

* To make coconut milk at home: Blend one cup of hot water with one cup of fresh coconut or dried unsweetened shredded coconut. Let it stand for 30 minutes, then strain the liquid for use in this and other recipes.

Green Chard and Cauliflower Curry

> 1 lb. green chard, finely chopped and steamed
> 3/4 cup cauliflower, cut into 1/2-inch pieces and
>   steamed
> 1 tablespoon ghee
> 1/2 teaspoon fennel seeds
> 1/2 teaspoon Pitta Churna
> 1/2 teaspoon turmeric
> salt to taste

Sauté fennel seeds and Pitta Churna in ghee. Add steamed vegetables, turmeric and salt. Heat for several minutes.

Serves 2 to 3.

Mixed Vegetable Curry (See recipe in Section Two, page 43)

Puréed Spinach

> 1 lb. fresh spinach or green chard
> 2 teaspoons ghee
> 2 pinches nutmeg
> salt to taste

Chop spinach or chard and steam until cooked. Blend in a blender for about 15 seconds, until it is lightly blended into a thick paste. Place on a serving dish and add a little ghee, nutmeg and salt.

Option: Add 1/2 cup of cubed panir (see recipe on page 31).

Serves 2 to 3.

Sweet Squash Curry

> 1 1/2 cups butternut squash or pumpkin
> 1 tablespoon ghee
> 1/2 teaspoon fresh ginger root, grated

3/4 teaspoon Pitta Churna

1 teaspoon dried unsweetened shredded
  coconut

1 tablespoon cilantro leaves, minced

1 tablespoon raisins, soaked for one hour or
  more

1 pinch nutmeg

1 teaspoon brown sugar

salt to taste

Bake or steam squash. Remove skin and gently mash. Set aside.

Sauté fresh ginger, Pitta Churna and coconut in ghee, stirring continuously. Add squash, cilantro, raisins and nutmeg. Stir in the sugar and salt. Cook for five more minutes.

Serves 2.

Grains

Basmati Rice (See recipe in Section Two, page 46)

Coconut Rice

1/2 cup white basmati rice

1 cup water

1 teaspoon sugar

1/4 teaspoon cardamom seeds, crushed

1 tablespoon ghee

1/8 cup dried unsweetened shredded coconut

Rinse rice well and add to boiling water. Add sugar and cardamom. Cover pot and allow to simmer for about 20 minutes.

In a separate pot, lightly brown coconut in ghee, stirring continuously. When the rice is done stir in the coconut and steam with the lid on for another three minutes. Remove from the heat and serve.

Serves 2 to 3.

Raisin Almond Rice

3/4 cup white basmati rice

1 1/2 cups water

2 tablespoons yellow raisins

2 teaspoons ghee

1/4 teaspoon coriander seeds, crushed

1 tablespoon blanched almonds, slivered

1/4 cup panir, cut into small cubes (see recipe on page 31)

1/4 teaspoon salt

2 tablespoons cilantro leaves, finely chopped

Rinse rice thoroughly. Cook in fresh water with raisins for about 20 minutes.

In a separate pan, sauté the coriander, almonds and panir in ghee. Place the rice in a serving dish and add the panir mixture. Add salt and cilantro and lightly mix.

Serves 2 to 3.

Rice Pilaf (See recipe in Section Two, page 49)

Sweet Rice

3/4 cup white basmati rice

1 1/2 cups water

2 tablespoons raisins

1 teaspoon coriander seeds, freshly ground

1/4 teaspoon cardamom seeds, freshly ground

1/4 teaspoon fennel seeds

1/2 teaspoon sugar

1/4 teaspoon salt

1 tablespoon dried unsweetened shredded
    coconut, dry-roasted

Rinse rice thoroughly. Boil fresh water and add the rice, raisins, spices and sugar. Lower heat and simmer for 20 minutes. Add salt at the end of cooking. Garnish with coconut before serving.

Serves 2 to 3.

Salads

Couscous Salad

1 cup couscous
1 1/2 cups water
1/4 cup peas, cooked
2 tablespoons red bell pepper, minced and
    steamed
1 teaspoon fresh parsley, minced
1 teaspoon fresh mint leaves, minced
1 teaspoon cilantro leaves, minced
1/2 teaspoon cumin seeds, freshly ground
salt and pepper to taste
2 tablespoons olive oil
1/4 cup fresh orange juice

Boil water and add couscous. Bring to a second boil, cover pan and remove from the heat. Let it sit for ten minutes.

Put couscous into a serving dish and allow to cool. Stir in the rest of the ingredients except the olive oil and orange juice. Mix the olive oil and orange juice together and then pour over the salad. Let the salad marinate for about 15 minutes before serving.

Serves 3.

Cucumber Salad

    1/2 cup cucumber, peeled and chopped

    1/4 cup cilantro leaves, minced

    2 tablespoons red, orange or yellow bell pepper, finely chopped

    1/2 teaspoon fresh ginger root, grated

    1/2 teaspoon cumin seeds, dry-roasted and crushed

    1/2 teaspoon coriander seeds, crushed

    2 teaspoons olive oil

    1/4 teaspoon salt

Toss together cucumber, cilantro, bell pepper and fresh ginger. Add the cumin seeds, coriander seeds, olive oil and salt, and mix well. Let it sit for 15 minutes so the flavors will meld.

Serves 2.

Grated Vegetable Salad (See recipe in Section Two, page 52)

Mixed Green Salad

    1 cup red bib lettuce

    1/2 cup dandelion greens

    1/2 cup arugula

    1/4 cup watercress

    1/8 cup fresh basil leaves

    1 tablespoon sunflower seeds or pine nuts, dry-roasted

    1/2 cup panir, crumbled (optional) (see recipe on page 31)

    2 tablespoons olive oil

    salt and pepper to taste

Tear all the greens into bite-sized pieces. Add the roasted seeds or nuts and panir. Toss with olive oil, salt and pepper.

Serves 2 to 3.

Chutneys

Apple Date Chutney

> 1/3 cup fresh mint leaves
> 2 tablespoons apple juice
> 1/2 cup dates, soaked overnight (or simmered
>   for 15 minutes)
> 1/2 apple, peeled and sliced
> 2 teaspoons Pitta Churna
> 1 teaspoon sugar
> 1/2 teaspoon rock salt
> 1 pinch turmeric

Blend mint leaves in a blender with apple juice. Then add dates and apple and blend briefly until barely mixed. Add the rest of the ingredients and blend briefly again, until just mixed.

Serves 2 to 3.

Fresh Mango Chutney (See recipe in Section Two, page 54)

Mint Coconut Chutney

> 1/2 cup fresh mint leaves
> 1/2 cup fresh coconut, grated (or dried
>   unsweetened shredded coconut)
> 1 tablespoon ghee
> 1 tablespoon fresh ginger root, grated
> 1 pinch hing
> 1/2 cup yogurt
> 1 tablespoon sugar
> 1/4 teaspoon salt
> 1 pinch black pepper

Sauté fresh ginger and hing in ghee. Add coconut and sauté until golden, stirring continuously.

Put mixture in a blender or food processor along with the mint leaves, yogurt, sugar, salt and pepper. Blend until it becomes a thick paste.

Serves 2 to 3.

Pineapple Chutney (See recipe in Section Two, page 55)

Cilantro and Avocado Chutney

1/2 cup cilantro leaves, minced

2 tablespoons water

1/2 cup raisins, soaked overnight (or simmered for 15 minutes)

1/2 cup avocado, cut into pieces

1/2 cup yogurt

1 tablespoon fresh coconut, grated (or dried unsweetened shredded coconut)

2 tablespoons lime juice

2 teaspoons sugar

1/2 teaspoon cumin seeds, dry-roasted

1/2 teaspoon rock salt

1 pinch turmeric

Blend cilantro leaves with a little water in a blender. Add raisins to the cilantro mixture and continue to blend. Add the rest of the ingredients and blend briefly, until it forms a thick, smooth paste. Let the chutney sit for 15 minutes before serving.

Serves 2 to 3.

Breads

Chapati Flatbread (See recipe in Section Two, page 56)

Dosas (See recipe in Section Two, page 57)

Desserts

Apple and Rhubarb Cobbler
(See recipe in Section Two, page 58)

Baked Pears

>   4 pears (Comice, Bartlett or Anjou varieties)
>   1/4 cup brown sugar
>   2 teaspoons ghee
>   1 teaspoon crystallized ginger, minced
>   1/2 teaspoon lemon peel, grated

Preheat your oven to 350 degrees Fahrenheit. Slice pears in half and remove skin, core and seeds. Place the pears face down in a buttered baking dish. Sprinkle the rest of the ingredients on top and bake for about 15 minutes or until the pears are soft.

Serves 3 to 4.

Dried Fruit Balls

>   3/4 cup dried dates, cut into pieces
>   3/4 cup dried figs, cut into pieces
>   1/2 cup raisins
>   1/2 cup sugar
>   2 pinches nutmeg
>   2 pinches clove
>   1 pinch cinnamon
>   2 cups water
>   3/4 cup blanched almonds, chopped
>   3/4 cup dried unsweetened shredded coconut

Boil all the ingredients together, except for the almonds and coconut. Reduce heat and simmer for about 20 minutes, until the fruit is soft and water is almost gone.

Remove from the heat and stir in the almonds and coconut. Allow the mixture to cool until it can be handled comfortably, and then form into balls. Roll the balls in coconut, if you like.

Serves 3 to 4.

Melon Salad

1/2 cup watermelon, cut into pieces or balls

1/2 cup honeydew melon, cut into pieces or balls

1/4 cup cantaloupe, cut into pieces or balls

a few sprigs of fresh mint leaves, finely minced

1/4 teaspoon ground cardamom

1/8 teaspoon nutmeg

Mix ingredients together and serve at room temperature. Serves 2.

Rice Pudding (See recipe in Section Two, page 61)

Tapioca Pudding (See recipe in Section Two, page 62)

Beverages

Digestive Lassi (See recipe in Section Two, page 62)

Indian Tea

1/2 cup milk

1 teaspoon fresh ginger root, grated

1/2 teaspoon fennel seeds

1/2 teaspoon cardamom seeds

1 cup water

1 bag black tea

2 teaspoons sugar or to taste

Slowly bring milk and spices to a boil, and simmer for ten minutes.

While milk is simmering, boil the water in a separate pan. Remove the pan from the heat and steep the tea bag in the hot water for five minutes.

Remove tea bag and add the milk, with the spices strained out of it, to the tea. Then add sugar and simmer for five more minutes.

Serves 1.

Mint Barley Drink

1/2 cup barley (use whole-grain organic barley
   for the best flavor)
3 cups water
1/8 cup fresh mint leaves
2 teaspoons sugar or to taste

Bring water to a boil. Add barley and cook on a soft boil for about one hour. Remove barley by draining the water into another pot. Allow the barley water to cool.

Put two cups of barley water, mint leaves and sugar in a blender. Blend until smooth. This makes a particularly cooling, soothing drink for Pitta.

Serves 2.

Mint Lassi (See recipe in Section Two, page 62)

Rose Lassi (See recipe in Section Two, page 62)

Royal Mango Lassi (See recipe in Section Two, page 63)

Warm Milk and Cardamom

> 1 cup milk
> 1 teaspoon sugar
> 1/4 teaspoon ground cardamom
> 3 threads saffron, crumbled

Slowly bring milk to a boil with sugar, cardamom and saffron. Gently boil for a few minutes. Remove from the heat and cool to drinking temperature. This is a good drink to have about a half hour before going to bed.

Options:

For breakfast try adding Almond Energy Drink (available at health food stores) instead of sugar.

For a gentle laxative effect, add a little melted ghee (one-half teaspoon or one teaspoon) to the milk and drink it when it is still very warm.

Serves 1.

Menu Suggestions

Breakfast

Toast with butter and Rose Petal Conserve

Warm Milk and Cardamom with ghee (see page 87)

Puffed rice cereal with milk

Dates stuffed with a small amount of ghee

Pitta Tea

Stewed apples or pears cooked with cloves

Cooked oatmeal

Pitta Tea

Rice Pudding (see page 61)

Raja's Cup

Chapati Flatbread (see page 56)

Warm Milk with Almond Energy Drink (see page 63)

Lunch

Mixed Bean Soup (see page 71)

Green Chard and Cauliflower Curry (see page 77)

Coconut Rice (see page 78)

Mixed Green Salad (see page 81)

Fresh Mango Chutney (see page 54)

Chapati Flatbread (see page 56)

Rose Lassi (see page 62)

Garbanzo Bean Dal (see page 69)

Puréed Spinach (see page 77)

Raisin Almond Rice (see page 79)

Cilantro and Avocado Chutney (see page 83)

Melon Salad (see page 85)

Brown Lentil Dal (see page 69)

Fresh Pea and Panir Curry (see page 75)

Sweet Rice (see page 79)
Royal Mango Lassi (see page 63)

Dinner

Split Mung Dal (see page 37)
Rice Pilaf (see page 49)
Chapati Flatbread (see page 56)
Cream of Spinach Curry (see page 74)
Basmati Rice (see page 46)
Sambar Dal (see page 36)
Dosas (see page 57)
Rice and Dal (see page 36)
Baked Pears (see page 84)

SECTION FOUR

Kapha-Balancing Recipes

Bean Soups

Black Bean Dal

> 1/2 cup black beans, rinsed well and soaked
>   overnight
> 1 1/2 cups water (or more for thinner dal)
> 1/2 bay leaf
> 1 tablespoon ghee or olive oil
> 2 teaspoons fresh ginger root, grated
> 1/4 cup red bell pepper, chopped
> 1 teaspoon cumin seeds, dry-roasted
> 1/4 teaspoon turmeric
> salt and pepper to taste
> 1 teaspoon cilantro leaves, minced

Drain beans and rinse again. Bring beans to a boil in fresh water along with the bay leaf, then reduce heat to medium low.

In a separate frying pan, sauté fresh ginger in ghee or oil. Add red pepper and sauté for a few minutes. Add mixture to the beans.

Dry-roast cumin seeds and add to the dal with turmeric and pepper. Cook for about 40 minutes or until beans are tender. Add salt and pepper at the end of cooking. Garnish with cilantro before serving.

Serves 2 to 3.

Lentil and Barley Dal

> 1/2 cup brown lentils
> 2 tablespoons barley
> 2 1/2 cups water (or more for thinner dal)
> 1 bay leaf

1/4 cup potato, diced

1/4 cup green beans, cut into 1/2-inch pieces

1/2 tomato, diced

1 tablespoon carrots, sliced

1 tablespoon fresh parsley, minced

1/2 teaspoon dried basil (or 1 teaspoon fresh
  basil, minced)

1/4 teaspoon dried oregano (or 1/2 teaspoon
  fresh oregano, minced)

1/4 teaspoon dried marjoram

1/2 teaspoon salt

1/4 teaspoon pepper

2 tablespoons olive oil

1/2 teaspoon black mustard seeds

1 tablespoon cilantro leaves, minced

Rinse lentils and barley thoroughly. Bring them to a boil in water. Cover and reduce heat to medium low. Add the bay leaf.

Cook for 15 minutes, then add vegetables and parsley. Cook for another 30 minutes or until lentils, barley and vegetables are done.

At the end of cooking, add basil, oregano, marjoram, salt and pepper. In a separate pan, pop mustard seeds in hot oil and add to the dal. Garnish with cilantro before serving.

Serves 2 to 3.

Lima Bean Dal

1/2 cup lima beans, rinsed well and soaked overnight

1 1/2 cups water (or more for thinner dal)

1/2 bay leaf

1/4 teaspoon turmeric

1/2 teaspoon ground fenugreek

1/4 teaspoon black pepper

1 tablespoon ghee

1 teaspoon fresh ginger root, grated
1/4 cup potato, diced
1/4 cup celery or spinach, chopped
1/4 teaspoon lemon rind, grated
1/2 teaspoon salt

Drain beans and rinse again. Add beans to fresh boiling water along with the bay leaf, turmeric, fenugreek and pepper. Cover and simmer over medium-low heat.

In a separate pan, sauté fresh ginger, potato and celery or spinach in ghee. Then add to lima beans with lemon rind. Cook for about 40 minutes or until vegetables and beans are tender. Add salt at the end of cooking.

Serves 2 to 3.

Pinto Bean Dal

1/2 cup pinto beans, rinsed well and soaked
    overnight
1 1/2 cups water (or more for thinner dal)
1/2 bay leaf
1/4 teaspoon turmeric
1 pinch cinnamon
2 tablespoons ghee or olive oil
1/2 teaspoon black mustard seeds
2 teaspoons fresh ginger root, grated
1/4 cup red bell pepper, chopped
1 1/2 teaspoons cumin seeds, dry-roasted
1/2 teaspoon salt
1 tablespoon cilantro leaves, chopped

Drain beans and rinse again. Add beans to fresh boiling water, then reduce heat to medium low. Add bay leaf, turmeric and cinnamon.

In a separate pan, pop the mustard seeds in hot ghee or oil. As they start to pop, add fresh ginger, then red pepper.

Sauté for a few minutes. Add fried mixture to the beans.

Crush the dry-roasted cumin seeds and add them to the beans. Continue cooking until the beans are very soft. Add salt at the end of cooking and cilantro just before serving.

Serves 2 to 3.

Rice and Dal (See recipe in Section Two, page 36)

Split Mung Dal (See recipe in Section Two, page 37)

Yellow Split Pea Dal

> 1/2 cup yellow split peas
> 1 1/2 cups water (or more for thinner dal)
> 1/2 bay leaf
> 1 tablespoon ghee or olive oil
> 1/4 teaspoon black mustard seeds
> 1/4 cup cabbage, diced
> 1 tomato, diced
> 1 teaspoon Kapha Churna
> 1/4 teaspoon turmeric
> 1/4 teaspoon salt

Rinse peas well. Boil fresh water and add peas and bay leaf. Cover pot and reduce heat to low.

In a separate pan, heat ghee or oil and sauté mustard seeds until they start to pop. Then add the cabbage and sauté for several minutes. Add tomato, Kapha Churna and turmeric. Cook for another two or three minutes.

Add vegetable mixture to the dal and simmer until peas are done. Add salt at the end of cooking.

Serves 2 to 3.

Vegetables

Brussels Sprouts and Potato Curry

> 2 cups Brussels sprouts, cut in half
> 1/2 cup potatoes, cubed
> 2 teaspoons ghee
> 1 teaspoon cumin seeds
> 1/2 teaspoon dried ginger powder
> 1/4 teaspoon turmeric
> 1 pinch clove
> 1 pinch hing
> salt and pepper to taste

Steam Brussels sprouts and potatoes until almost done.

In a separate pan, sauté cumin seeds, ginger, turmeric, clove and hing in ghee. Add steamed vegetables and stir until they are coated with spices. Cook for about five minutes until vegetables are tender. Add salt and pepper to taste.

Serves 2 to 3.

Cabbage and Pea Curry

> 1 1/2 cups cabbage, cut into 1/4-inch slices
> 1/4 cup fresh snow peas
> 2 teaspoons ghee or olive oil
> 1/2 teaspoon black mustard seeds
> 1 teaspoon cumin seeds
> 1 teaspoon fresh ginger root, grated
> 1 dash of hing
> 1 small tomato, diced
> 1/4 teaspoon turmeric
> salt and black pepper to taste

Lightly steam cabbage and peas and set aside.

In a large frying pan, pop the mustard seeds in hot ghee

or oil, then add cumin seeds, fresh ginger and hing. Then add
steamed vegetables, tomato and turmeric. Sauté for a few
minutes. Add salt and pepper to taste.

Serves 2.

Cabbage Soup

> 2 cups cabbage, sliced
>
> 2 tomatoes, chopped
>
> 1 potato, peeled and diced
>
> 1/4 cup parsnips, sliced
>
> 1 carrot, sliced
>
> 2 teaspoons fresh parsley, minced
>
> 2 teaspoons olive oil
>
> 1/2 cup onion, sliced
>
> 1 clove garlic, minced (optional)
>
> 1 1/2 teaspoons Kapha Churna (or 1 teaspoon
>   dried ginger powder, 1/2 teaspoon black
>   pepper, 1/4 teaspoon ground cumin and 1/4
>   teaspoon turmeric)
>
> water
>
> salt to taste

In a large pan, sauté onion and garlic in olive oil. Add
Kapha Churna (or alternate spices) and sauté briefly. Add
all the vegetables and parsley and enough water to cover the
top of the vegetables.

Bring to a boil and then reduce heat to low. Cover and
cook for about an hour and a half. Add salt at the end of
cooking.

Serves 3.

Daikon Root and Kale Curry

1 cup daikon root, cubed
2 cups kale, chopped
2 teaspoons ghee
3/4 teaspoon ground cumin
1/2 teaspoon dried ginger powder
1/4 teaspoon turmeric
1 pinch ground clove
1/2 cup water
salt to taste
Lightly steam the daikon.

In a large frying pan, sauté spices in ghee. Add steamed daikon and sauté for several minutes. Add kale and water. Cover the pan and cook until vegetables are done. Add salt at the end of cooking.

Serves 2 to 3.

Gingered Cauliflower

1 head cauliflower, cut into flowerets
2 teaspoons ghee
2 teaspoons fresh ginger root, grated
1/2 teaspoon ground cumin
1/4 teaspoon turmeric
1 pinch clove
1 small tomato, cubed
salt and pepper to taste

In a large frying pan, sauté the fresh ginger in ghee. Add cumin, turmeric and clove. Then add the cauliflower and stir until it is coated in spices. Reduce heat to medium low and cover pan. Stir often to prevent cauliflower from sticking to the pan.

Add tomato and continue cooking until the cauliflower is tender. Add salt and pepper to taste.

Serves 3

Green Bean and Cauliflower Curry

    1 cup green beans, cut into 1/2-inch pieces
    1 cup cauliflower, cut into flowerets
    1 tablespoon ghee
    1/4 teaspoon fenugreek seeds
    1 teaspoon cumin seeds
    1/2 teaspoon fresh ginger root, grated
    1/2 teaspoon turmeric
    1 small tomato, diced
    salt and pepper to taste

Heat ghee in a large skillet. Sauté fenugreek seeds first, then add cumin seeds. Add fresh ginger and cook for about a minute. Add cauliflower and green beans and sauté briefly. Reduce heat and add turmeric and tomato. Cover and cook until vegetables are tender. Add salt and pepper to taste.
    Serves 2 to 3.

Okra and Potato Curry

    1 cup okra, cut into 1/2-inch pieces
    1 cup potatoes, cubed
    2 teaspoons ghee
    1/4 teaspoon fenugreek seeds
    1 teaspoon cumin seeds
    1/4 teaspoon fresh ginger root, grated
    1/4 teaspoon garlic, minced
    1 tablespoon onion, minced
    1/4 teaspoon turmeric
    salt and pepper to taste

Steam potatoes until almost done.

In a separate pan, sauté in ghee the following ingredients (in this order): fenugreek seeds, cumin seeds, fresh ginger, garlic, onion and turmeric. Add okra and sauté for about five minutes.

Add steamed potatoes and continue cooking until the okra is tender. (While cooking, don't put the lid on; otherwise, it will become sticky.) Add salt and pepper at the end of cooking.

Serves 2.

Spiced Collard Greens

1 lb. collard greens, cut into strips
1 tablespoon olive oil
1-2 cloves garlic, minced
1 tablespoon raisins or dried cranberries
a few tablespoons of water
salt and pepper to taste

Rinse collard greens well. Discard the thick middle stem when you cut them into strips. Boil greens for ten minutes, drain and set aside.

In a large frying pan, heat oil and sauté the garlic. Add raisins or cranberries, collard greens and water. Cook with lid on until greens are tender. Add salt and pepper at the end of cooking.

Serves 2 to 3.

Grains

Barley Sauté

    1 cup barley
    3 cups water
    2 teaspoons ghee
    1/2 teaspoon mustard seeds
    1/2 teaspoon fenugreek seeds
    1 teaspoon cumin seeds
    1 teaspoon fresh ginger root, minced
    1/2 teaspoon turmeric
    2 tablespoons red bell pepper, minced
    1 teaspoon fresh parsley, minced
    2 teaspoons fresh basil, minced
    1/4 teaspoon salt

Rinse barley thoroughly. Bring fresh water to a boil, then add barley. Cover and reduce heat to low. Cook for 45 minutes or until barley is done.

In a separate frying pan, heat ghee. Add the mustard seeds and fenugreek seeds. When they begin to pop, add cumin seeds, then fresh ginger. Sauté until ginger turns golden. Then add turmeric and red pepper.

When the red pepper is semi-soft (about three minutes), add the cooked barley, parsley, basil and salt. Sauté for a few more minutes.

Serves 3.

Basmati Rice (See recipe in Section Two, page 46)

Millet Pilaf

1 cup millet
1 tablespoon ghee or olive oil
1 teaspoon fresh ginger root, grated
2 tablespoons carrots, sliced
2 tablespoons green beans, cut into 1/2-inch
    pieces
2 tablespoons potato, diced
2 tablespoons peas
1 teaspoon Kapha Churna
3 cups water
salt and black pepper to taste

Rinse millet thoroughly.

In a large pan, stir-fry the fresh ginger and vegetables in ghee or oil for two or three minutes. Add millet, Kapha Churna and water. Bring to a boil. Cover and simmer for 20 minutes, or until millet is done and vegetables are tender. Add salt and pepper to taste.

Serves 3.

Rice Pilaf (See recipe in Section Two, page 49)

Spiced Quinoa

1 cup quinoa
2 cups water
2 teaspoons carrots, finely chopped
1 teaspoon Kapha Churna (or 1/2 teaspoon
    ground cumin, 1/2 teaspoon ground corian-
    der, 1/2 teaspoon dried ginger powder, 1/4
    teaspoon turmeric and 1 pinch hing)
1/8 teaspoon salt
1 teaspoon fresh parsley, minced

Rinse the quinoa and spread out on a paper towel to dry.

Then preheat your cooking pot. Add dry quinoa and allow it to lightly toast, stirring often to prevent burning.

Add water, carrots and Kapha Churna (or alternate spices). Bring to a boil. Cover and reduce heat to a simmer. Cook for about 15 minutes or until the quinoa has absorbed all of the water.

Add salt at the end of cooking. Remove from the heat and let stand uncovered for five minutes. Fluff with a fork and garnish with parsley before serving.

Serves 3.

Three-Grain Salad

1/4 cup quinoa
1/8 cup wild rice
1/8 cup barley
1 1/2 cups water
1/2 cup corn kernels
1/8 cup fresh peas or snow peas
1 tablespoon red bell pepper, minced
1 tablespoon olive oil
1 teaspoon lemon juice
2 teaspoons fresh parsley, minced
1/2 teaspoon fresh thyme leaves, or a dash of
    dry thyme
salt and pepper to taste

Rinse each grain separately. Bring water to a boil and add wild rice and barley. Reduce heat to low, cover and cook for about 30 minutes.

Add quinoa to the grain pot and continue to cook for another 30 minutes, or until all the grains are done. Then allow them to cool.

In a separate pot, steam the vegetables until tender. Then combine grains, vegetables, olive oil, lemon juice, parsley, thyme, salt and pepper.

Serves 2 to 3.

Vegetable Couscous

> 2/3 cup couscous
> 1 cup water
> 2 tablespoons apple, peeled and cut into small
>   pieces
> 2 tablespoons fresh orange juice
> 1 tablespoon dried currants
> 1 tablespoon peas, steamed
> 1 teaspoon green onion, minced (optional)
> 1/2 teaspoon fresh ginger root, grated
> salt and pepper to taste

Bring water to a boil. Add couscous. Bring to a second boil, cover pan and remove from the heat. Let it stand for about ten minutes.

Put couscous into a serving bowl and mix in the rest of the ingredients.

Serves 2 to 3.

Salads

Arugula and Pear Salad

> 1 cup arugula greens, torn into small pieces
> 1/2 cup red leaf lettuce, torn into small pieces
> 1/2 pear, peeled and diced
> a few croutons
> black pepper to taste (freshly ground)

> *Dressing:*
> 2 teaspoons mustard
> 2 teaspoons raw honey
> 1 tablespoon yogurt
> 2 pinches clove
> 1/4 cup water

Arrange salad ingredients. Then mix dressing
ingredients together and pour over salad.
Serves 2 to 3.

Blanched Vegetable Salad

1 cup asparagus, cut into 1/2-inch pieces
1/2 cup broccoli, cut into pieces
1/2 cup cauliflower, cut into pieces

Dressing:
1 tablespoon olive oil
1 teaspoon lemon juice
1/4 teaspoon cumin seeds, dry-roasted
1/4 teaspoon dried ginger powder
1/8 teaspoon black pepper
1 dash of clove

Blanch vegetables by pouring boiling water over them
and allowing them to sit in the hot water for a few minutes
before draining.

Combine the dressing ingredients separately and pour
over the vegetables.

Serves 2 to 3.

Broccoli Orzo Salad

1 cup cooked orzo pasta
1 1/2 cups broccoli, cut into pieces
1 tablespoon olive oil
1 teaspoon lemon juice
1/2 teaspoon garlic, minced
2 teaspoons raisins (optional)
1/8 teaspoon black pepper
salt to taste

Cook orzo pasta for about 8 minutes, until it is cooked
al dente.

Blanch the broccoli pieces by pouring boiling water over them and allowing them to sit in the hot water for a few minutes before draining.

Combine pasta, broccoli and the other ingredients. Mix together gently. Let the salad rest for 15 minutes before serving.

Serves 2 to 3.

Daikon Soba Salad

1 1/2 cups cooked soba noodles (Asian buckwheat noodles)
1/2 cup daikon root, cut into small pieces
1/4 cup carrots, grated
1/8 cup celery, finely chopped
1 teaspoon fresh ginger root, grated
1 teaspoon green onion, chopped (optional)
2 teaspoons olive oil
1 teaspoon lemon juice
1/8 teaspoon black pepper
salt to taste

Cook soba noodles for about seven minutes. Drain and cool until room temperature. Add vegetables and other ingredients. Mix well.

Serves 2 to 3.

Grated Vegetable Salad (See recipe in Section Two, page 52)

Jicama Salad

1/2 cup jicama, diced
1/2 cup apples, diced
1/8 cup celery, chopped
1 tablespoon raisins or currants

Dressing:
1/2 cup water
1/4 cup yogurt
2 teaspoons raw honey
1 teaspoon Kapha Churna

Mix salad ingredients. Then mix dressing ingredients together and pour over salad.
Serves 2 to 3.

Chutneys

Apple Pear Chutney

1/4 cup apple, chopped
1/4 cup pear, chopped
2 tablespoons raisins
2 tablespoons water
1 teaspoon ghee
1 teaspoon black mustard seeds
1 teaspoon fresh ginger root, grated
1/8 teaspoon hing
1/8 teaspoon cinnamon
1/8 teaspoon clove
1 dash of salt
1 teaspoon raw honey (optional)

Sauté the mustard seeds in ghee until they pop. Add fresh ginger and hing. Add fruit, raisins and water and cook on low heat until soft. Then add the cinnamon, clove and salt.
Allow to cool. Add honey if desired.
Serves 2 to 3.

Papaya Chutney

> 1 cup fresh or dried papaya, cut into small
>   pieces
> 1 teaspoon ghee
> 1/2 teaspoon black mustard seeds
> 2 teaspoons fresh ginger root, grated
> 2 teaspoons lemon juice
> 1 teaspoon sugar
> 1 dash of salt
> 2 teaspoons raw honey

Sauté mustard seeds in ghee until they start to pop. Add fresh ginger and continue to sauté. Add papaya, lemon juice, sugar and salt. Cover and simmer until fruit is soft. (If you use dried papaya, add 1/4 cup water.)

Remove from the heat and allow to cool. Then add honey.

Serves 2 to 3.

Breads

Chapati Flatbread (See recipe in Section Two, page 56)

Dosas (See recipe in Section Two, page 57)

Vegetable Pancakes

> 3/4 cup chickpea flour
> 1/4 cup wheat flour
> 1/2 teaspoon salt
> 2 teaspoons Kapha Churna
> 1/2 cup water (or more as needed)
> 1/2 tomato, diced
> 2 tablespoons carrots, grated
> 2 tablespoons mung bean sprouts

1 teaspoon fresh ginger root, grated
1 teaspoon onion, minced (optional)
1 teaspoon cilantro leaves, minced
ghee

Mix the two flours, salt, Kapha Churna and water to make a smooth pancake batter. Add tomato, carrots, sprouts, fresh ginger, onion and cilantro.

Heat ghee in a large skillet and pour about two table-spoons of batter into the skillet to form each pancake. Use a spoon to spread the batter evenly. Fry each side for about five minutes over medium-high heat until golden. Serve with chutney.

This recipe makes about four pancakes.

Desserts

Baked Pears (See recipe in Section Three, page 84)

Fruit Salad with Blueberry Sauce

1 apple, peeled and diced
1 pear, peeled and diced
1/2 cup blueberries
1/2 cup raspberries
1 pinch clove
1 pinch cinnamon
1 pinch nutmeg
Blueberry sauce:
1/2 cup blueberries
2 teaspoons raw honey

Mix fruit and spices together. Blend the blueberries for the sauce in a blender. Stir in the raw honey. Pour sauce over the fruit.

Serves 3 to 4.

Quick Apple Crisp

> 4 cups apples, peeled and sliced
> 1/4 cup raisins or currants
> 1/4 cup apple or pear juice
> 1 teaspoon cinnamon
> 1/4 teaspoon nutmeg
> 1 pinch dried ginger powder
> 2 tablespoons brown sugar or raw honey
> 1/2 cup dried unsweetened shredded coconut,
>   dry-roasted
> 1/2 cup granola (any kind)

Combine apples, raisins, juice and spices in a medium-sized pot. Cook over medium heat for about fifteen minutes until the apples are semi-soft.

Remove from the heat and allow to cool. Add sugar or honey and stir well. Scoop into dessert bowls. Top with a tablespoon of coconut and granola.

Serves 3 to 4.

Tapioca Pudding (See recipe in Section Two, page 62)

Beverages

Digestive Lassi (See recipe in Section Two, page 62)

Indian Tea (See recipe in Section Three, page 85)

Sweet Lassi

> 1/3 cup yogurt
> 1 cup water
> 1 pinch clove
> 2 teaspoons raw honey

Blend yogurt, water and clove. Then stir in honey and serve.

Serves 1 to 2.

Warm Milk and Ginger (See recipe in Section Two, page 63)

Menu Suggestions

Breakfast

> Chapati Flatbread with honey and cinnamon
>   (see page 56)
> Warm Milk and Ginger (see page 63)
> Cooked oatmeal with raisins
> Kapha Tea
> Stewed apples or pears cooked with cloves
> Cornmeal mush
> Raja's Cup
> Quick Apple Crisp (see page 111)
> Chapati Flatbread (see page 56)
> Indian Tea (see page 85)

Lunch

> Black Bean Dal (see page 93)
> Spiced Collard Greens (see page 101)
> Basmati Rice (see page 46)
> Ginger Preserve

Chapati Flatbread (see page 56)

Baked Pears (see page 84)

Pinto Bean Dal (see page 95)

Green Bean and Cauliflower Curry (see page 100)

Millet Pilaf (see page 103)

Arugula and Pear Salad (see page 105)

Split Mung Dal (see page 37)

Brussels Sprouts and Potato Curry (see page 97)

Rice Pilaf (see page 49)

Apple Pear Chutney (see page 108)

Dinner

Lentil and Barley Dal (see page 93)

Chapati Flatbread (see page 56)

Yellow Split Pea Dal (see page 96)

Three-Grain Salad (see page 104)

Cabbage and Pea Curry (see page 97)

Split Mung Dal (see page 37)

Cabbage Soup (see page 98)

Vegetable Pancakes (see page 58)

SOURCES FOR
MORE INFORMATION

Maharishi Vedic Medicine

Centers Offering Programs in Maharishi Vedic Medicine

The following centers offer courses, conferences, treatment programs and individual consultations with doctors who are trained in Maharishi Vedic Medicine.

In the United States:

Maharishi Vedic Medical Center
5504 Edson Lane
Bethesda, Maryland 20852
Phone: 301-770-5690
Fax: 301-770-5694
E-mail: vedicdc@aol.com

Maharishi Vedic Health Center
The Center for Chronic Disorders and
    Prevention
679 George Hill Road
Lancaster, Massachusetts 01523
Phone: 978-365-4549
Web site: www.LancasterHealth.com

The Raj
1734 Jasmine Avenue
Fairfield, Iowa 52556
Phone: 800-248-9050 or 641-472-9580
Fax: 641-472-2496
E-mail: theraj@lisco.com
Web site: www.theraj.com

In Canada:

> Maharishi Ayur-Veda College
> Paterson House
> Maharishi Vedic Health Centre
> 500 Wilbrod Street
> Ottawa, Ontario K1N 6N2
> Phone: 877-385-5350
> Fax: 613-565-6546
> Web site: www.patersonhouse.com
>
> *More information is available on the web:*
> www. Maharishi-medical.com
> www.vedic-health.com

Maharishi Vedic Universities, Colleges, Schools and Centers

Maharishi Vedic Universities, Colleges, Schools and Centers offer courses and educational programs in Maharishi Vedic Medicine. They are located in many cities in both the United States and Canada. If you are unable to find a listing in your local telephone directory or from directory assistance, call toll-free 888-532-7686 or see the following web site: www.Maharishi.org.

Health Education Short Courses for the Whole Population

These 16-hour courses are offered at Maharishi Vedic Universities, Colleges, Schools and Centers. Full descriptions of these courses can be found at the following web site: www.Maharishi.org.

1. Human Physiology: Expression of Veda and the Vedic Literature
2. Good Health through Prevention

3. The Maharishi Yoga™ Program
4. Self-Pulse Reading Course for Prevention
5. Diet, Digestion and Nutrition
6. Maharishi Vedic Astrology℠ Overview
7. Maharishi Vedic Architecture

Degree Programs

Bachelor of Science program in Maharishi Vedic Medicine and Ph.D. program in physiology with specialization in Maharishi Vedic Medicine:

Maharishi University of Management
College of Maharishi Vedic Medicine
1000 North Fourth Street
Fairfield, Iowa 52557
Phone: 641-472-4600
Fax: 641-472-4610
E-mail: cmvm@mum.edu
Web site: www.mum.edu/cmvm

Master of Science program for health professionals in Maharishi Vedic Medicine:

Maharishi College of Vedic Medicine
2721 Arizona Street, NE
Albuquerque, New Mexico 87110
Phone: 888-895-2614 or 505-830-0415
Fax: 505-830-0538
E-mail: mcvmnm@aol.com
Web site: www.mcvmnm.org

Maharishi Open University

This global university delivers the total knowledge of Natural Law, including the knowledge of Maharishi Vedic Medicine, via a worldwide network of eight satellites to the people of every country.

E-mail: MOU@Maharishi.net
Web site: www.MOU.org

Where to Order Maharishi Ayur-Veda Herbal Formulas and Other Products

For a wide range of Maharishi Ayur-Veda herbal formulas, health care products, personal care products, food products, massage oils, aroma oils and diffusers, books, tapes and CDs, contact:

Maharishi Ayurveda Products International, Inc.
1068 Elkton Drive
Colorado Springs, Colorado 80907
Phone: 800-255-8332 or 719-260-5500
Fax: 719-260-7400
E-mail: info@mapi.com
Web site: www.mapi.com

For organic dals and grains by mail order, contact:

Delicious Dal and Company
300 East Broadway
Fairfield, Iowa 52556
Phone: 641-470-1507

How to Locate a Physician Trained in Maharishi Vedic Medicine

Physicians trained in Maharishi Vedic Medicine give individual recommendations based on profound diagnostic techniques such as Maharishi Ayur-Veda pulse diagnosis. For the doctor nearest you, contact your nearest Maharishi Vedic University, College, School or Center, or one of the centers offering programs in Maharishi Vedic Medicine listed previously.

Dr. Kumuda Reddy and Dr. Janardhan Reddy may be reached at:

Samhita Productions
P.O. Box 2164
Kensington, Maryland 20891-2164
Web site: www.allhealthyfamily.com
1 866 ReddyMD (1 866 733-3963) or
301 770-0610

How to Locate a Teacher of the *Transcendental Meditation* Technique

The Transcendental Meditation technique is a simple, natural, effortless procedure practiced for fifteen to twenty minutes morning and evening, sitting comfortably with eyes closed. It is considered the most important aspect of Maharishi Vedic Medicine. Over 600 scientific studies conducted at more than 200 universities and research institutions in 30 countries have demonstrated the profound benefits of this technique for mind, body, behavior and environment. For more information, call 888-LEARN-TM (888-532-7686) or see the following web site: www.tm.org.

The *Maharishi Vedic Astrology and Maharishi Yagya*^{SM} Programs

The Maharishi Vedic Astrology program analyzes the influences that come to us from our cosmic counterparts-the sun, moon, planets and far-distant galaxies. Through a consultation with an expert in Maharishi Vedic Astrology we can identify positive and negative influences coming from our extended environment and take proper precautions to avert any negativity or ill health.

A Maharishi Vedic Astrology consultation identifies a problem but does not solve it. For this we have the Maharishi Yagya program. This program gives us precise Vedic performances that restore balance in the functioning of Natural Law. When you consult an expert in Maharishi Vedic Astrology, you automatically receive recommendations for any necessary Maharishi Yagya performances.

Conducted before the danger arises, these performances help neutralize negative influences. They generate a positive influence that restores harmony between the individual and the cosmos so that life proceeds more smoothly. Maharishi Yagya performances may also be used to enhance influences that are already positive and bring even better health and greater success.

The *Maharishi Vedic Astrology
     and Maharishi Yagya* Programs
P.O. Box 1839
Hillsboro, New Hampshire 03244
Phone: 800-483-2234 or 603-588-4235
Fax: 603-588-4249
E-mail: MaharishiYagya@Maharishi.net
Web site: www.yagya.org

Maharishi Sthapatya Veda® Design

Sthapatya comes from the word meaning "to establish." Veda means "knowledge." The Maharishi Sthapatya Veda program gives the knowledge of establishment-how to establish yourself and your environment in accord with all the Laws of Nature.

The Maharishi Sthapatya Veda program is a perfect system of design for countries, cities, towns and neighborhoods, as well as individual homes and workplaces. It gives dimensions, formulas and orientations so that each human environment is structured in harmony with the cosmos and gives ideal support for health, happiness and peace.

To learn more about Maharishi Sthapatya Veda design, contact:

Maharishi Global Construction
500 North Third Street, Suite 110
Fairfield, Iowa 52556
Phone: 641-472-9605
Fax: 641-472-9083
E-mail: reception@MGC-Vastu.com
Web site: www.Vedahouse.com

Maharishi's Global Country of World Peace

In October 2000, Maharishi Mahesh Yogi inaugurated a Global Country of World Peace and crowned His Majesty King Nader Raam as its first sovereign ruler. Citizenship of the Global Country of World Peace is open to all the peace-loving people of the world. Anyone who wishes to become a citizen is cordially invited to fill out a brief form at the following web site: www.globalcountry.org.

Recommended Reading

Maharishi Mahesh Yogi

Maharishi Mahesh Yogi is the founder of Maharishi Vedic Medicine and is regarded as the world's foremost scientist in the field of consciousness. His Transcendental Meditation technique, taught in all parts of the world since 1958, is the most widely practiced and extensively researched program of self-development in the world.

Maharishi has restored the true meaning and significance of the age-old Vedic Literature and has organized it in the form of a complete science and technology of consciousness available to all. To maintain the purity of this Vedic tradition of knowledge generation after generation, he has established a global network of universities and an organization with more than 1,200 centers in 108 countries.

Here is a partial listing of his many books.

Life Supported by Natural Law. Washington, D.C.:
   Age of Enlightenment Press, 1986.

*Maharishi Mahesh Yogi on the Bhagavad-Gita: A
   New Translation and Commentary, Chapters* 1-6.
   New York: Penguin Books, 1990.

*Science of Being and Art of Living: Transcendental
   Meditation. New York*: Penguin Books, 1995.

*Maharishi Forum of Natural Law and National Law
   for Doctors.* India: Age of Enlightenment
   Publications, 1995.

Celebrating Perfection in Education. India: Age of
   Enlightenment Publications, 1997.

Scientific Research on Maharishi Vedic Medicine

Scientific Research on Maharishi's Transcendental Meditation and TM-Sidhi Program: Collected Papers, Volumes 1-6, available through Maharishi University of Management Press, Press Distribution, DB 1155, Fairfield, Iowa 52557. Phone: 800-831-6523 or 641-472-1101. Fax: 641-472-1122. E-mail: mum-press@mum.edu. Web site: www.mum.edu/press/welcome.

Scientific Research on the Maharishi Transcendental Meditation and TM-Sidhi Programs Including Yogic Flying: A Brief Summary of 600 Studies. Fairfield, Iowa: Maharishi University of Management Press, 2000.

Other Books

Nader, Tony, M.D., Ph.D. *Human Physiology: Expression of Veda and the Vedic Literature.* Vlodrop, The Netherlands: Maharishi Vedic University Press, 1994.

Denniston, Denise. *The TM Book: How to Enjoy the Rest of Your Life.* Fairfield, Iowa: Fairfield Press, 1986.

Fagan, John. *Genetic Engineering: The Hazards, Vedic Engineering: The Solutions.* Fairfield, Iowa: Maharishi International University Press, 1995.

Lonsdorf, Nancy, M.D., Veronica Butler, M.D., and Melanie Brown, Ph.D. *A Woman's Best Medicine: Health, Happiness, and Long Life through Ayur-Veda.* New York: Jeremy P. Tarcher/Putnam, 1993.

O'Connell, David, and Charles N. Alexander. *Self Recovery: Treating Addictions Using Transcendental Meditation and Maharishi Ayur-Veda.* New York: Haworth Press, 1994.

Olson, Helena and Roland. *His Holiness Maharishi Mahesh Yogi: A Living Saint for the New Millennium*. Schenectady, New York: Samhita Productions, 2001.

Roth, Robert. *Maharishi Mahesh Yogi's Transcendental Meditation*. New York: Donald I. Fine, 1994.

Sharma, Hari, M.D. *Awakening Nature's Healing Intelligence: Expanding Ayurveda through the Maharishi Vedic Approach to Health*. Twin Lakes, Wisconsin: Lotus Press, 1997.

Sharma, Hari, M.D. and Christopher Clark, M.D. *Contemporary Ayurveda: Medicine and Research in Maharishi Ayur-Veda*. Philadelphia: Churchill Livingstone, a Division of Harcourt Brace & Company, 1998.

Wallace, R. Keith. *The Neurophysiology of Enlightenment*. Fairfield, Iowa: Maharishi International University Press, 1986.

Wallace, R. Keith. *The Physiology of Consciousness*. Fairfield, Iowa: Maharishi International University Press, 1993.

Many of these books and others are available from Maharishi University of Management Press, Press Distribution, DB 1155, Fairfield, Iowa 52557. Phone: 800-831-6523 or 641-472-1101. Fax: 641-472-1122. E-mail: mumpress@mum.edu. Web site: www. mum.edu/press/welcome.

Books by Dr. Kumuda Reddy

Reddy, Kumuda, M.D. and Stan Kendz. *Forever Healthy: Introduction to Maharishi Ayur-Veda Health Care*. Rochester, New York: Samhita Enterprises, Inc., 1997.

Reddy, Kumuda, M.D., Linda Egenes, M.A., and Margaret Mullins, M.S.N., F.N.P. *For a Blissful Baby: Healthy and Happy Pregnancy with Maharishi Vedic Medicine*. Schenectady, New York: Samhita Productions, 1999.

Reddy, Kumuda, M.D., Thomas Egenes and Linda Egenes, M.A. *All Love Flows to the Self: Eternal Stories from the Upanishads*. Schenectady, New York: Samhita Productions, 1999.

Reddy, Kumuda, M.D., Janardhan Reddy, M.D. and Sandra Willbanks, M.A. *Golden Transition: Menopause Made Easy through Maharishi Vedic Medicine*. Schenectady, New York: Samhita Productions, 2002.

Reddy, Kumuda, M.D., and Linda Egenes, M.A. *Conquering Chronic Disease through Maharishi Vedic Medicine*. Schenectady, New York: Samhita Productions, 2002.

Dr. Reddy's books can be ordered from Lantern Books, P.O. Box 960 Herndon, VA 20172-0960. Phone: 800-856-8664. Fax: 703-661-1501.

Email: anthroposophicmail@presswarehouse.com. Web site: www.lanternbooks.com or Dr. Reddy's web site: www.allhealthyfamily.com.

About the Authors

Dr. Kumuda Reddy and Dr. Janardhan Reddy are a married team committed to bringing the time-tested knowledge of Maharishi Vedic Medicine to the modern world. Both are medical doctors with over 25 years of experience each in the practice of conventional Western medicine. Trained in Maharishi Vedic Medicine, they have found that this natural, holistic system complements Western care and has the potential to solve many of the health problems we face today.

Dr. Kumuda Reddy completed her residency and fellowship at Mt. Sinai Hospital, New York. For many years she was a faculty member at Albany Medical College. For ten years she practiced Maharishi Vedic Medicine in upstate New York. Currently she is practicing in Bethesda, Maryland.

She has coauthored four books on Maharishi Vedic Medicine: Forever Healthy: Introduction to Maharishi Ayur-Veda Health Care, For a Blissful Baby: Healthy and Happy Pregnancy with Maharishi Vedic Medicine, Conquering Chronic Disease through Maharishi Vedic Medicine, and Golden Transition: Menopause Made Easy through Maharishi Vedic Medicine. She also coauthored a book of stories from the Upanishads entitled All Love Flows to the Self and a series of children's stories called the Timeless Wisdom Series, based on traditional Indian stories that she first heard as a child.

Dr. Janardhan Reddy has extensive experience in various clinical fields, including urology, general surgery and neurosurgery. He completed his residency in urology and was in urological private practice for almost two decades.

Together, the Reddys write and give lectures on Maharishi Vedic Medicine. Their forthcoming books include *Living Life Free from Pain: Treating Joint Pain and Arthritis,*

Muscle Pain and Fibromyalgia with Maharishi Vedic Medicine and *Let's Keep Our Children Healthy and Happy with Maharishi Vedic Medicine*.

The Reddys are active community members and devoted to their extended family. They have three children: Sundeep, Hima and Suma. They live and work in Bethesda, Maryland.

Bonita Pedersen has been an instructor in Maharishi Ayur-Veda health care and a teacher of the Transcendental Meditation program since 1989. For many years she was Director of the Maharishi Ayur-Veda Health Center in Seattle, Washington. Currently, she is a health technician and cooking instructor at The Raj, a premier Ayurvedic health center located in Fairfield, Iowa that specializes in Maharishi Rejuvenation[SM] therapies. Bonita lives in Fairfield with her husband Geir Ketil and her daughter Anna.